Rutland Water Nature Reserve

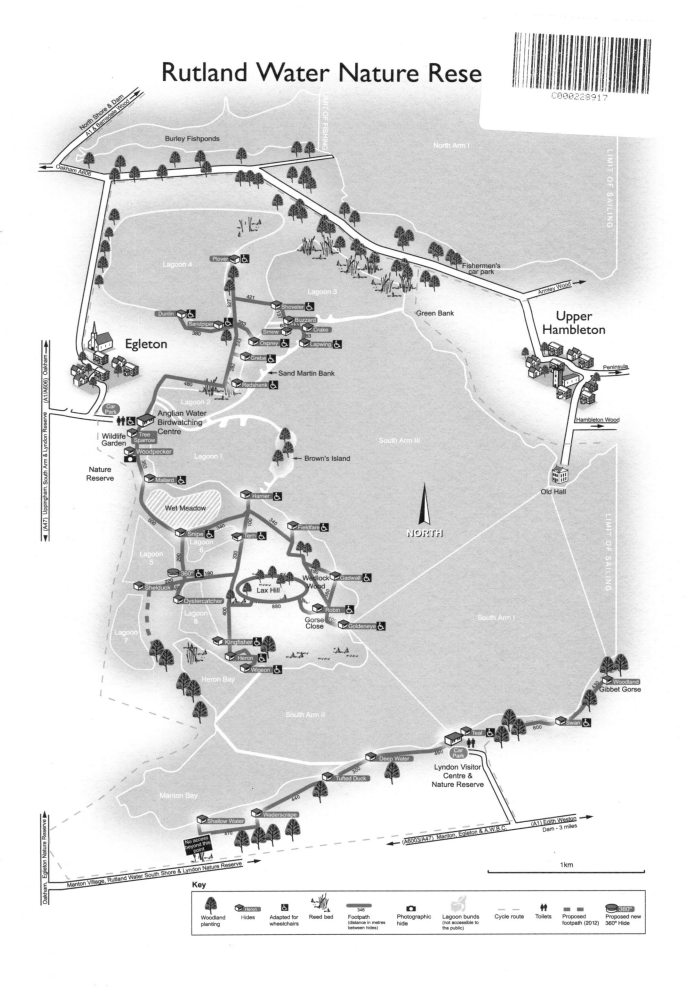

NORTH

Egleton

Upper Hambleton

Burley Fishponds

North Arm I

Fishermen's car park

Green Bank

Lagoon 4

Lagoon 3

Plover

Shoveler

Buzzard

Dunlin

Sandpiper

Smew

Crake

Osprey

Lapwing

Grebe

Sand Martin Bank

Redshank

Lagoon 2

Car Park

Anglian Water Birdwatching Centre

Tree Sparrow

Wildlife Garden

Woodpecker

Nature Reserve

Mallard

Lagoon 1

Brown's Island

South Arm III

Old Hall

Peninsula

Hambleton Wood

Armley Wood

Harrier

Wet Meadow

Fieldfare

Snipe

Tern

Lagoon 6

Lagoon 5

360°

Shelduck

Gadwall

Wedlock Wood

Lax Hill

Oystercatcher

Robin

Lagoon 8

Gorse Close

Goldeneye

South Arm I

Lagoon 7

Kingfisher

Heron

Wigeon

Heron Bay

South Arm II

Woodland Gibbet Gorse

Swan

Teal

Car Park

Deep Water

Lyndon Visitor Centre & Nature Reserve

Tufted Duck

Manton Bay

Shallow Water

Waderscrape

No access beyond this point

(A1) Edith Weston
Dam - 3 miles

(A6003/A47) Manton, Egleton & A.W.B.C.

Oakham, Egleton Nature Reserve

Manton Village, Rutland Water South Shore & Lyndon Nature Reserve

North Shore & Dam
A1 & Barnsdale Wood

Oakham A606

(A1/A606) Oakham

(A47) Uppingham, South Arm & Lyndon Reserve

LIMIT OF FISHING

LIMIT OF SAILING

1km

Key

Woodland planting	Hides	Adapted for wheelchairs	Reed bed	346 Footpath (distance in metres between hides)	Photographic hide	Lagoon bunds (not accessible to the public)	Cycle route	Toilets	Proposed footpath (2012)	Proposed new 360° Hide

THE
RUTLAND WATER
OSPREYS

Leicestershire
& Rutland
Wildlife Trust

love
every
drop.
anglianwater

THE
RUTLAND WATER
OSPREYS

Text by Tim Mackrill,
Tim Appleton and Helen McIntyre

Photographs and illustrations by John Wright

BLOOMSBURY

LONDON · NEW DELHI · NEW YORK · SYDNEY

First published in 2013

Copyright © 2013 Anglian Water and the Leicestershire & Rutland Wildlife Trust

The rights of Anglian Water and the Leicestershire & Rutland Wildlife Trust to be identified as the authors of this
work have been asserted by them in accordance with the Copyright, Designs and Patents Act 1988.

Bloomsbury Publishing Plc, 50 Bedford Square, London WC1B 3DP
Bloomsbury USA, 175 Fifth Avenue, New York, NY 10010

www.bloomsbury.com
www.bloomsburyusa.com

Bloomsbury Publishing, London, New Delhi, New York and Sydney

A CIP catalogue record for this book is available from the British Library
Library of Congress Cataloging-in-Publication Data has been applied for

Commissioning Editor: Julie Bailey
Design by Julie Dando at Fluke Art

UK ISBN (print) 978-1-4081-7414-2

Printed in China by C&C Offset Printing Co Ltd.

10 9 8 7 6 5 4 3 2 1

MIX
Paper from
responsible sources
FSC® C008047

Contents

Foreword

When I look back over the highlights of my working life so far, the Rutland Osprey Project provides some of the most special moments, so I am honoured to write a foreword for this excellent book. The project was not only an exciting and challenging exercise – aiming to restore the Osprey to the southern half of England – but it resulted, for me, in enduring friendships with a number of great people.

Following success with translocation projects involving sea eagles and Red Kites, I was sure that Ospreys could be restored in a similar way to England and Wales, as they had been in North America and in Tim Appleton Rutland Water had exactly the person to take such a project forward. I first met Tim in the 1980s when I visited Rutland Water to look at sites for building an Osprey nest, and admired his enthusiasm and his capable and proactive management of the brilliant Rutland Water Nature Reserve. In 1995, Tim again invited me to Rutland to talk about Ospreys, and we began planning the translocation of young Ospreys from Scotland. Fortunately, Steven Bolt of Anglia Water was equally enthusiastic and able to source sufficient funds, so we set about the task.

It was not easy to get permission for the project. Some bodies were against us from the start, and there was even concern that visitor numbers to Osprey centres in Scotland could be affected if Ospreys were to breed in England. Many others, though, were supportive, and Scottish Natural Heritage and English Nature finally gave us permission to proceed. Two more excellent people – Helen McIntyre and, later on, Tim Mackrill – arrived to run the project.

Landowners in the Scottish Highlands and the Forestry Commission graciously allowed me to collect young from nests on their lands. There followed a thrilling and exhausting six years, working alongside colleagues each summer to collect the chicks in Scotland before handing them over to Tim Appleton and his Osprey team to rear and release. These were great times. I vividly remember going to the first nest on 6 July 1996. Along with Joe Hayes, I collected the very first chick. Its mother was green J, which I went on to satellite tag in 1999. She winters in Extremadura and is still with us – in 2012 she was again back at the same place, rearing young.

In Scotland I awaited the call from Tim Appleton that an Osprey had returned from Africa. Three years later, in 1999, that call came, and I was as elated as the Rutland Team at the news. I couldn't wait to see the first nest with young. The Rutland Osprey Project has since gone from strength to strength, not only establishing an increasing population in the English Midlands but also restoring the Osprey to Wales. It has encouraged projects in Spain, Portugal and Italy. This book tells the Rutland Water story through the memories of Tim Appleton, Helen McIntyre and Tim Mackrill, and through the photographs and drawings of John Wright. John has taken the individual identification of Ospreys to a new level and has added greatly to our knowledge. I applaud Tim, Helen, Tim and John for their work in producing such an interesting and absorbing book and, of course, for their work on one of Britain's most successful wildlife projects.

Roy Dennis, MBE
Highland Foundation for Wildlife

The Osprey

SCIENTIFIC NAME   *Pandion haliaetus*

SIZE   55–62cm

WINGSPAN   145–180cm

WEIGHT   1.2–2kg

PLUMAGE   Brown upperparts contrast with white underside, with variable brown streaks on the breast. Head is white with a distinctive dark brown band running through the yellow eye. Females are generally larger and darker than males.

DIET   Exclusively fish, caught with specialised talons from on, or just beneath, the water's surface after a spectacular dive.

BREEDING AND LIFE EXPECTANCY   Most Ospreys do not breed until they are 3–5 years of age. They can live into their twenties and usually remain faithful to the same mate and nest site each year. Females usually lay a clutch of three eggs, which take 35–40 days to hatch. Young fledge when they are 7–8 weeks of age.

DISTRIBUTION AND POPULATION SIZE   Ospreys occur on every continent except Antarctica, with a world population of approximately 40,000 pairs, divided into three subspecies. The Australian or Eastern Osprey (*Pandion cristatus*) has recently been recognised as a separate species. Numbers are now increasing in Europe and North America, where the species suffered population declines caused by pesticides, persecution and habitat loss. Within Europe, the main stronghold is Scandinavia, with large numbers also breeding in Russia.

MIGRATION   European and North American subspecies are migratory, while the Caribbean race is sedentary. The majority of European Ospreys winter in sub-Saharan Africa, in coastal areas or inland near rivers and lakes.

An Introduction to the Project

The recent history of the Osprey in the UK is a great conservation success story. Having been persecuted to extinction in England by the Victorians, the population in Scotland also dwindled in the early part of the 20th century. For almost 30 years there were only sporadic breeding records, but from the late 1950s the population began to recover again. Thanks to a concerted conservation effort these magnificent raptors have since recovered well and the population in Scotland now stands at more than 260 breeding pairs.

As the Scottish population increased, so too did sightings of migrant and summering birds in England. Of the various places they were recorded passing through, one was a vast new reservoir, Rutland Water.

Constructed in the 1970s midway between Peterborough and Leicester, Rutland Water covers more than 3,100 acres and has 17 miles of shoreline. A nature reserve occupies 9 miles of shoreline at the western end, which is managed by the Leicestershire and Rutland Wildlife Trust on behalf of the owners of the reservoir, Anglian Water. This nature reserve has become one of the most important inland sites for birds in the UK. In excess of 25,000 wildfowl are regularly recorded in early winter, including internationally important populations of Gadwall and Shoveler. The reservoir was designated a Ramsar site – a wetland of international importance – in 1991.

In 1996 Anglian Water, the Leicestershire and Rutland Wildlife Trust and the Highland Foundation for Wildlife began a groundbreaking project to restore a breeding population of Ospreys centred on the reservoir. Over the course of six years between 1996 and 2001, 64 six-week-old Ospreys were translocated from north-east Scotland to Rutland, with a further 11 birds moved in 2005.

More than 15 years after it began, the translocation project has completely changed the distribution map of

The view across Manton Bay from Shallow Water hide. This spot is one of the best places to see Ospreys at Rutland Water.

Ospreys in the UK. A breeding population is now well established in the Rutland Water area and the translocation has also resulted in the recolonisation of Wales. Furthermore, groundbreaking satellite-tracking studies have revealed new and exciting information about the birds' epic migration to West Africa.

This book tells the full story of the project, from initial conception on a cold winter's day at Rutland Water to the translocation of the first chicks from Scotland, and the establishment of a breeding population. In many ways the story is as much about the people involved as the birds themselves.

It's been a privilege to be involved in the return of these marvellous birds to the skies of central England and we hope you enjoy reading about the highs and lows of the past 20 years as much as we've enjoyed writing about them.

Tim Mackrill, Tim Appleton and Helen McIntyre

A Who's Who of the Rutland Osprey Project

RINGING AND NAMING THE OSPREYS

All 75 Ospreys that were translocated to Rutland Water between 1996 and 2001 were fitted with a metal British Trust for Ornithology (BTO) ring on one leg and a larger Darvic ring, with a unique alphanumeric code, on the other. All of the juveniles reared in nests since 2001 have been ringed in the same way. Apart from in 1996 and 1997, the Darvic ring has always been placed on the bird's right leg, with Scottish birds ringed on the left. It's possible to read the inscription on the Darvic ring in the field using a high-powered telescope from a distance of up to 300 metres. In this book all the birds are referred to by their Darvic ring number, with the year they were translocated/fledged in brackets. For instance 03(97) was translocated to Rutland Water in 1997 and fitted with a white Darvic ring bearing the inscription 03. 5R(04) fledged from a nest in Rutland in 2004 and was ringed with a Darvic ring bearing the inscription 5R.

SOME KEY BIRDS

03(97) (left) was translocated to Rutland Water from Scotland in 1997. He returned to Rutland in 1999 and successfully bred with an unringed female for the first time in 2001. They were the first Ospreys to rear young in central England for more than 150 years. 03(97) has continued to breed at Site B, his nest on private land close to Rutland Water, each year since, raising a total of 27 chicks with three different females. Several of his offspring have returned to breed in Rutland and 03(08) bred for the first time at Cors Dyfi in Mid Wales in 2011.

08(97) (right) was translocated to Rutland Water from Scotland in 1997. He was the first translocated Osprey to return to Rutland, in May 1999. Despite attracting at least eight different females to his nest in Manton Bay, he didn't breed until 2007, when he raised two chicks with 5N(04). After their nest failed in 2008 the pair moved to a site on private land, Site N, and raised two chicks in 2009 and 2010. Sadly 08(97) disappeared in suspicious circumstances in May 2011.

09(98) (above) was translocated to Rutland Water from Scotland in 1998. He returned to Rutland for the first time in 2000 and bred in 2012, with 5N(04) at Site N. He was fitted with a satellite transmitter in 2011, allowing us to chart his migration to the coast of Senegal.

5R(04) (above), offspring of 03(97) and 05(00), fledged from Site B in 2004. 5R(04) was the first wild-fledged male to return to Rutland, in June 2006. In 2010, he raised three chicks in Manton Bay with an unringed Scottish female. They were the first breeding pair not to include a translocated bird and have raised young each year since.

05(00) (above) was translocated to Rutland Water in 2000 and returned for the first time two years later. In 2003 she paired up with 03(97) at Site B and became the first translocated female to breed successfully. Over the course of six summers, she raised a total of 17 chicks at Site B with 03(97). Sadly she failed to return in 2009.

5N(04), daughter of 03(97) and 05(00) and sister of 5R(04), fledged from Site B in 2004. She was the first wild-fledged female to return to Rutland, in July 2006. Next summer she became the first wild-fledged chick to breed, raising two chicks with 08(97) in Manton Bay. She continued to breed with 08(97), latterly at Site N, until his disappearance in 2011. After 08(97)'s disappearance she paired up with 09(98) at Site N.

AW(06) (left), offspring of 03(97) and 05(00), fledged from Site B in 2006. He returned to Rutland in 2008 and bred for the first time in 2010, at a nest on private land known as Site O, with a Scottish female from Argyll. He raised six chicks in two years and was fitted with a satellite transmitter in 2011. Sadly he died at his wintering site on the Ivory Coast in February 2012.

THE OSPREY TEAM

TIM MACKRILL

Tim's first involvement with the project was as a 15-year-old volunteer in 1997. Later he was employed as a member of the project team during university holidays while he completed a degree in ecology at the University of East Anglia. After graduating, Tim returned to Rutland and has been managing the project since 2006. He is also carrying out a PhD on Ospreys in conjunction with Leicester University.

JOHN WRIGHT

John Wright, a skilled all-round naturalist, has been employed as the project's Field Officer since 2002. In the last decade he has developed a unique knowledge of the Rutland Ospreys that is reflected in his superb artwork and photography.

TIM APPLETON

Having previously worked for Sir Peter Scott at Slimbridge, Tim has been managing Rutland Water Nature Reserve since its conception in the 1970s, overseeing its development into one of the most outstanding places for birds in the UK. Tim is also the co-organiser of the annual Birdfair, which has raised more than £2.5 million for conservation projects worldwide since 1989. He was awarded an MBE for his services to nature conservation in 2004.

HELEN MCINTYRE

Having graduated with a higher degree in landscape ecology, Helen worked in environmental consultancy, focusing on ecological restoration projects. She managed the translocation project between 1996 and 2002, overseeing the day-to-day care and monitoring of the birds.

ROY DENNIS

Roy has been instrumental in helping Ospreys to return to the UK. His lifelong involvement began when he was appointed as an Osprey warden at Loch Garten in 1960. He went on to become the RSPB's Highland Officer before setting up the Highland Foundation for Wildlife in 1995. Having been closely involved in the reintroduction of White-tailed Eagles and Red Kites to Scotland, Roy was one of the driving forces behind the Rutland translocation and remains an advocate of proactive conservation. In 1992 he was awarded an MBE for services to nature conservation in Scotland and in 2004 he was voted the RSPB Golden Eagle Award winner for the person who had done most for nature conservation in Scotland in the last 100 years.

ANDY BROWN

Andy is Anglian Water's Head of Sustainability and is the day-to-day link between the project and the water company. He has been involved with the project, through Anglian Water, since 1996.

Ospreys Return to the UK

A Chequered History

Ospreys would have graced the skies of Rutland long before the first authenticated records in the late 1800s, but wouldn't have had the same welcome they receive today. They would have been seen as a serious threat to the carefully managed fish ponds of local landowners, which provided a much-needed source of protein for the table. Early persecution would not have been devastating to the populations of breeding Ospreys, but as guns became more accessible and reliable this would undoubtedly have accounted for the demise of the species. This persecution was exacerbated by Victorian collectors, who were less concerned about the fish eaten by the Ospreys than they were about stuffing Ospreys into glass display cases and collecting their eggs to be set out in silk-lined boxes.

Inevitably the numbers of Ospreys throughout Britain started to decline, especially in the more populated and readily accessible regions of England. There are many early references in English literature suggesting that Ospreys were breeding in the south: Cornwall, Devon, the Isle of Wight, Somerset, Sussex and even Lundy Island are all mentioned. However, the last recorded breeding in England was around 1847 in the Somerset Levels. Although they were lost to England, Ospreys continued to breed in Scotland, but in ever-declining numbers and driven to the most remote lochs and wildernesses. Unfortunately the Victorians were not ones to give up their quest for the species and eventually Ospreys ceased to breed in the British Isles.

The view along the North Arm of Rutland Water. The reservoir has a surface area of 3,100 acres.

The demise of the Osprey largely occurred before the advent of the county avifaunas, so it wasn't until Charles Haines published *Notes on the Birds of Rutland* in 1907 that we get our first authenticated records of their presence in the county. He describes the Osprey as an occasional visitor on its spring passage to the Burley and Exton Fishponds. Burley Fishponds, now part of the Rutland Water Nature Reserve, was to play a pivotal role in the return of the Ospreys to Rutland more than 100 years after the first official record. Haines reports that: 'A bird came on the same day, staying 30 hours on each occasion from 1878 to 1883.' Sadly, like so many Ospreys of that period, it was shot in 1884 at Coleorton in Leicestershire. The next sighting was on 2 April 1886 and then again in 1894. Nearby Exton Pond hosted a very early migrating Osprey on 21 February and 5 March 1898. There was a stuffed Osprey at Burley House near Oakham, probably shot at one of the fish ponds. The final paragraph in Haines describes how the late Mr R. Tyron watched a bird fishing at the Burley Lower Pond: '…it dropped like a stone with its wings slightly open, then rose from the water with what might have been a Jack in its claws'. This is a familiar sight to thousands of visitors who flock to a number of breeding sites in Britain, now that attitudes to raptor conservation have thankfully changed and for the most part birds are left to nest and raise their young in peace.

This change dates back to the famous pair of Ospreys that bred at Loch Garten in Strathspey in the Scottish Highlands in the 1950s. These breeding attempts were initially kept secret, as egg collectors were still hell-bent on stealing their prized quarries and Osprey eggs provided a huge challenge and reward for these misguided 'criminals'. There were several attempts to rob nests but the then Director of the RSPB in Scotland, George Watson, had the foresight to set up Operation Osprey – a group of dedicated RSPB wardens and volunteers – to protect the nesting birds. In 1959 this pioneering pair of Ospreys successfully raised young and for the first time in ornithological history visitors were invited to view the birds on the nest. More than 14,000 people came to see the birds – the birth of birding ecotourism as we know it today.

As the years went by so the populations of Ospreys increased in Scotland, leading inevitably to many more sightings elsewhere in the UK as birds migrated northwards in the spring, then returned in the autumn to their wintering grounds in Africa.

In the mid-1970s a huge new reservoir was being constructed in the East Midlands. This would primarily provide water but there were also progressive plans to incorporate in the design a range of recreational activities and to create the first purpose-built nature reserve on a reservoir. There were already a number of established reserves on older reservoirs but these had been 'bolted on' later, whereas the new Rutland Water would make conservation a priority from the outset. The Leicestershire and Rutland Wildlife Trust were charged with the overall responsibility of managing the new reserve on behalf of the reservoir's owners, Anglian Water. This partnership would see the reservoir become a Site of Special Scientific Interest (SSSI), a Ramsar site and a Special Protection Area, making it the most outstanding inland reserve in Britain and demonstrating the value of a commercial company and a conservation organisation working together in harmony.

The next avifauna, covering the years from 1940 to 1974, makes no specific mention of Ospreys in Rutland, but Terry Mitcham's *The Birds of Rutland and its Reservoirs*, published in 1984, contains the first modern record of an Osprey visiting Rutland – at Eyebrook Reservoir in April 1955. There followed 11 further sightings through to the flooding of Rutland Water in 1976, and from then onwards the impact of this new body of water was evident, as Ospreys have been sighted annually ever since. Throughout the late 1970s and 1980s the number of records at Rutland Water continued to increase in parallel with the expanding Scottish populations. Always looking at ways in which new birds might be attracted to the reserve to breed, a rather ambitious attempt was made in 1986 by Chris Park, the then assistant warden.

Chris Park building the reserve's first artificial Osprey nest in May 1986.

Chris scaled one of the tallest trees on Lax Hill and – without any regard for self-preservation or modern-day safety equipment – skilfully constructed a nest on top of an exposed tree. Needless to say, Ospreys continued to pass over the reservoir without apparently taking a second glance at our attempt to persuade them to abandon their traditional strongholds in Scotland.

During the next ten years numbers fluctuated, ranging from single annual sightings to eight in 1988, nine in 1989 and 15 individuals in 1990. In 1992 there were 20 reports, but as in most previous years birds tended to stay only to fuel up on the Rutland fish before continuing their journeys. Then in 1994, it all changed with the arrival of a female Osprey on 15 May, followed by a male bird six days later on 21 May. Perhaps it was no coincidence that the birds favoured the same area – Burley Fishponds – as the ones observed a century earlier.

Over the following months, before their departure in early September, the birds were seen either together or separately on 95 occasions. Our inexperience and lack of knowledge about Ospreys and their breeding biology meant that (mistakenly) there was a growing anticipation that 'our pair' were bonding not just as a couple but also to their newly found home at Rutland Water. Our thoughts were already racing towards their assumed return the following spring.

Female Osprey perched near Burley Fishponds in 1994. She spent most of the summer at the reservoir, indicating she was either a two- or three-year-old bird.

AN EXCITING PLAN

As the winter progressed our thoughts turned to ways in which we might encourage the Ospreys should they return and nest. We had constructed nests in the past in what we considered to be suitable locations but nothing had happened. I had read about artificial platforms being successfully used by Ospreys in the USA so Roy Dennis, a world expert on the species, was invited down to see the reservoir and give advice on possible locations for nesting platforms. Roy had been crucial to the success of the expanding Osprey populations in Scotland, so we waited for his visit with high expectations. We were not disappointed – that first meeting in February 1995 was to form the foundation of a partnership between Anglian Water, the Leicestershire and Rutland Wildlife Trust and Roy, Director of the Highland Foundation for Wildlife, which would last to this day.

On the day of Roy's first visit, I met him together with Dr Stephen Bolt, Anglian Water's senior ecologist, and staff from the reserve. Five sites for platforms were quickly identified and Roy was so impressed by the partnership between the Trust and the water company that we soon started 'thinking outside the box' and the first ideas of a translocation scheme were aired. Rutland Water is England's largest reservoir, covering more than 3,100 acres, and as almost a third of the area is a nature reserve and the reservoir is full of fish, the site seemed to lend itself to such a scheme. The range of fish species is far greater than is found in any body of water in Scotland, so clearly it would offer Ospreys excellent fishing conditions as well as plenty of diverse habitats. We estimated that the reservoir could support eight to ten pairs of Ospreys and that its location in Eastern England would allow a natural spread of pairs to other lakes and reservoirs – and perhaps even to eventual recolonisation of the coastal areas around the Wash.

Roy returned on 16 March 1995 and with the help of the East Midlands Electricity Board, which arrived with a machine specifically designed for erecting electricity poles, five platforms were soon in place. The sites selected were chosen for their close proximity to the water and where any future occupied nest could be monitored without causing any disturbance – Burley Fishponds, Lagoon 3, Brown's Island, and two sites in the south arm of the reserve opposite the village of Manton.

As the following spring approached many an expectant eye was cast skywards, waiting for the moment our Ospreys would return after their long northern migration. Despite a number of false alarms time marched on and our fears – fuelled by Roy Dennis's prediction/advice – started to become a reality. The female bird eventually arrived but, true to form, the presumably Scottish-bred male was more than likely seeking out a new territory close to his natal site 500 miles further north.

The Jnr Marsh Harrier was hunting around Lagoon 2.

Ad ♀ Osprey (unringed)
Manton Bay
20·8·97

Migrant Scottish Ospreys often stop off at Rutland for a few days to feed and rest on their flight south each autumn. In 1997 an adult female spent time in Manton Bay with the newly released translocated juveniles.

The idea of the translocation scheme was gathering pace and when news came through that Anglian Water had agreed to support the programme financially it was time to start consulting with the licensing bodies in both England and Scotland. A project of this nature would eventually require a licence from Scottish Natural Heritage (SNH) to remove Osprey chicks from their nests and a second licence from English Nature (now Natural England), to hold wild birds in captivity before their release.

I wrote a brief outline and sent it to Dr Phil Grice, the licensing officer at English Nature based in nearby Peterborough, outlining our aims and objectives and requesting a meeting. The initial response was encouraging but, as we expected, there would be a mountain of work to do before we would get a decision. Phil's opening paragraph best sums up what lay ahead: 'The project is very interesting and a good deal of thought has obviously gone into the preparation of the proposal. However, there are a number of important issues that need to be fully addressed before English Nature could consider lending its support to such a project.' He then set out exactly what we would need to undertake in order to progress the project.

Our first and main objective was to prove that the strict International Union for Conservation of Nature (IUCN) criteria for reintroductions and translocations could be met. We would have to demonstrate that there was good historical evidence of former natural occurrence. Introducing a species into an area not known to be part of its former range would

Erecting a telegraph pole nest with the help of the local electrical company.

Roy Dennis spent two days at the reserve in March 1995 helping to build five new artificial nests.

set an extremely undesirable precedent for English Nature. We would also have to prove that, as the objectives of the UK Osprey Action Plan (OAP) did not consider translocation necessary, our project justified our proposed actions. The OAP aim was to target areas on the edge of the current range and provide artificial nesting platforms, and let natural colonisation take place throughout the UK.

We would also need to show that translocated Ospreys were not in danger of persecution, another of the IUCN criteria. Persecution might come not just from egg collectors – there could be problems at freshwater fisheries, where it was already perceived that an increase in the population of Cormorants was damaging fish stocks.

Another consideration would be researching the availability of suitable sites within the English Midlands, where Ospreys might eventually spread out from Rutland Water. It was clear that we would need to discuss the implications of this spread with landowners and other conservation partners.

Perhaps the most important requirement would be to demonstrate that the Scottish population could sustain the annual removal of young during the proposed five-year translocation period without suffering any adverse effect. There were 95 breeding pairs in Scotland in 1994, so there was naturally concern that removing young might slow down their natural expansion. Roy Dennis would need to undertake a

detailed analysis of the Scottish Osprey data on the population dynamics before any further progress could be considered.

English Nature was also concerned that there must be long-term monitoring and reporting. This was an essential part of the criteria, especially as this was essentially an experimental project – the success or failure would need to be assessed and lessons learnt that might help any future schemes.

One very positive outcome from these early communications that gave us hope the project might eventually get accepted was the recent reintroduction of Red Kites, which had proved highly successful and received universal approval from the birding community. Our project was thought timely because the Osprey and the Red Kite are regarded as the most popular birds of prey by the general public. It was likely that our project would generate favourable publicity for Ospreys, birds of prey and conservation in general. Birds of prey were under huge pressure from illegal trapping and poisoning, so any positive publicity would help enormously.

Phil Grice of English Nature had set us a number of daunting tasks but our enthusiasm and commitment to the project knew no bounds and we welcomed the challenge ahead. The first task was to be a meeting on 24 October 1995, involving interested parties from a number of NGOs that would eventually form the Rutland Water Osprey Steering Committee.

Rutland Water has become one of the best fly-fishing locations in the country. Anglian Water stocks the reservoir with over 100,000 trout each year.

The inaugural meeting saw Tim Appleton, Roy Dennis, Stephen Bolt from Anglian Water, Greg Mudge from SNH, Ian Carter and Phil Grice from English Nature, Michael Jeeves and Hugh Dixon from the Leicestershire and Rutland Wildlife Trust and Nicola Crockford from the RSPB sitting round the table. The meeting was very positive and we were able to fulfil several of the IUCN's criteria.

The historical evidence was discussed and although obviously Rutland Water didn't exist when Ospreys last bred in the area, it was agreed that they would have been part of the landscape before the onset of persecution and would have bred in the nearby fenlands, for example.

Roy had established that the mean annual rate of expansion of the Scottish population was around 3.4km per year. This suggested that, without exceptional pioneering pairs, it could take over 100 years for Ospreys to reach the East Midlands naturally, and colonisation of the rest of Britain might take twice as long, assuming expansion continued at the same rate.

We discussed the impact that Ospreys might have on commercial fisheries. Unlike the unpopular Cormorant, Ospreys do not occur in flocks and as a migrant species are only present in the UK from April to mid-September. Generally Ospreys are not viewed antagonistically by the majority of fishermen – in fact at Rutland Water our experience had been that fishermen were left disappointed

when they learnt that migrating Ospreys had been seen fishing at the reservoir but that they'd missed them. What's more, Rothiemurchus Fish Farm at Aviemore in the Highlands was actually encouraging Ospreys to fish at the farm, creating an unexpected local tourist attraction and benefitting the local economy.

Egg collectors were not seen as a serious threat – evidence from other reintroductions suggested that egg thieves are not interested in birds that are seen as 'tame'. The Rutland project would take place on a secure reserve with an established wardening scheme, full-time staff and an army of volunteers who would coordinate monitoring of nesting birds based on similar work in Scotland.

It was also noted that there were a number of suitable locations away from Rutland Water such as Eyebrook, Pitsford and Grafham Reservoirs, and many gravel pits where an expanding population of Ospreys could become established.

Professor Ian Newton, a world authority on birds of prey, had taken the view that removing 12 chicks per year from the Scottish population would have no impact on the population growth. Evidence from Scotland demonstrated that since 1954 the mean productivity had been 1.29 young per occupied nest and since 1990 it had been 1.34 young per nest. Throughout those intervening years there had been many attempts to rob nests, some successful, and yet the population had continued to grow. Earlier research by Alan

Poole, a world-renowned expert on Ospreys from the USA, had showed that 0.8 young per nest was required to maintain a stable population.

We discussed whether the runt of a brood would be a suitable candidate for translocation. In almost all cases the runt is the third chick to hatch and can suffer from food shortages. Given a 'second' chance there was plenty of evidence that this weaker chick would pick up through artificial feeding, whereas in the wild it would probably not survive alongside its siblings. Reducing the competition in the wild nest would result in more fish being available for the two remaining chicks, increasing their chances of survival. Scottish Ospreys don't have access to the range of fish species found in southern parts of Britain so future breeding birds south of the border should have a much greater chance to rear all three chicks to fledging.

Roy also explained at the meeting that studies showed that Ospreys prefer to nest in loose 'colonies' and the male bird almost always returns to its natal site, which would explain why our 1994 male, which was probably returning to the UK for the first time since its first migration, did not reappear in 1995. By removing male chicks from Scottish nests, it would firstly reduce the competition for established eyries there and secondly, males fledging from Rutland Water would hopefully return from Africa to Rutland as they would regard the reserve as their natal site.

Before the meeting we estimated that the minimum number of chicks to be translocated annually was 12. A higher number would clearly speed up the process of population growth, but we had to take into account the donor population and the amount of work involved in rearing the young birds. Establishing a population of Ospreys was clearly going to be much more difficult than it had been for both Red Kites and White-tailed Eagles (another reintroduction scheme). Unlike these two resident species, Ospreys undertake long annual migrations to Africa. Young first-time migrants don't return for at least two years, sometimes more. It may then be several years before successful pairing occurs and young are reared. Migration is full of pitfalls; inexperienced birds meet all types of obstacle, some natural, and others, such as shooting or becoming tangled in fishing nets, a direct result of man's actions.

The meeting proved to us that this would be no easy task, but we came away feeling that although there was still many a hurdle to overcome we were heading in the right direction. After the long and intense meeting we felt a need for some fresh air so the group was let loose on the reserve to inspect the nesting platforms raised earlier in the year. The work was just beginning.

On 31 January 1996 we received a letter that added enormous credibility to the project. Dr Mick Marquiss, a world expert on raptor ecology, had examined the data on breeding productivity in relation to the population increase in Scotland and our proposal to remove 12 young over a five-year period. In the early years of colonisation the population had increased rapidly, at an average of 11.9% per annum. In the very early years, when there were only a few breeding pairs, the annual increase varied from 0 to over 50%, but this stabilised at about 5% once the population reached 30 pairs. By the late 1980s there was a dramatic increase to 14% but that then fell to about 9%. Annual production varied widely in the early years but as the population increased the figure stabilised at around 1.29 young per pair. Further analysis suggested that taking into account the removal of the chicks, the Scottish population would continue to build and by 2000 there could be 157 pairs, producing more than 200 young.

In his letter Dr Marquiss summed up by saying: 'It seems on present evidence that the removal of 12 young in 1996 will have little if any detectable effect on subsequent population increase. Removals in subsequent years are likely to have even less effect because the expected production of young in those years will be much greater. Removal of 12 birds might reduce production by about 8.5% in 1996, but only 6% in 2000. In fact, the proposed removals would reduce production by far less because it is intended to use some nestlings that would otherwise perish. Going on the available evidence, if young were removed I believe we would hardly notice the difference.' In his final paragraph he draws a parallel with the Red Kite reintroduction, stating that: '...the artificial reintroduction of Ospreys in new areas with good foraging habitat will undoubtedly prove the most effective way of rapidly restoring both the range and abundance of Ospreys in Britain. Ospreys should be commonplace in Britain with a large, widespread population. Provided it is done carefully and diligently, the proposed reintroduction of Ospreys to England has every chance of success and will not be detrimental to the Scottish population. In the long term it will probably benefit the species in Britain as a whole.'

This letter gave us a huge boost and, we felt, fully justified our proposal, which was now ready to be submitted to SNH and English Nature, with copies going to all members of the steering group.

AN ANXIOUS WAIT

With the proposal now in the hands of the licensing bodies we could only wait and hope that we would get the approval. We knew there would be massive interest from birdwatchers and also from the press. The project proposal had been leaked to the *Daily Mail* a few weeks before and I had already spent several hours dealing with press enquiries.

Roy Dennis in Minnesota in 1996 during a fact-finding visit with Tim Appleton. The trip provided an opportunity to discuss the translocation techniques with Mark Martell and others. Ospreys were first released in Minnesota in 1984.

In the meantime we refurbished the existing nest platforms, while students from nearby Brooksby College – this time wearing full safety harnesses – climbed two suitable trees on Lax Hill and Gorse Close and constructed two fine new nests. Much to our dismay and disbelief these nests also proved ideal nesting sites for totally unexpected occupants: a pair of Canada Geese. Little did we know that this was a problem that was to cause the team many a headache in future years.

In mid-April a panel of experts met on behalf of SNH to consider our application. The group agreed unanimously that SNH should not object in principle, but that permission should only be granted following '...conclusion of consideration of these matters normally covered by a Population and Habitat Viability Assessment (PHVA)'.

This was a mixed blessing as, on the one hand, there were no objections, but we now had to undertake a PHVA. Had we been told this would be required when the steering committee first met the previous October, we could have sent it with our proposal. The response from SNH came while Roy and I were in America. We'd decided that while waiting for the outcome of our licence applications we would take up an offer from Mark Martell to visit the Raptor Center at the University of Minnesota. Mark, its raptor expert, had been responsible for the successful reintroduction of Ospreys to the twin cities of Minneapolis and St Paul. The USA was already well ahead of the field with translocation schemes, something still considered by most conservationists in the UK as a last resort. The state of Tennessee had led the way, starting way back in 1979, and similar projects had already taken place in 12 other states.

As had happened in Britain, Ospreys had disappeared as a breeding species throughout most of the state of Minnesota at the turn of the last century. Their translocation programme was initiated in 1984 and over subsequent years, through to 1993, 119 Osprey chicks were released at five locations around Minneapolis and St Paul. The Raptor Center recorded the first nesting attempt in 1986 and the first successful nesting followed in 1988, when two chicks fledged. By the time of our visit there were seven breeding pairs and 18 chicks had flown in the 1994 breeding season.

Our main aim was to look at the design of the Raptor Center's 'hacking' cages – or as we would later call them the release pens – and the methods they used when feeding young chicks and caring for nestlings before release.

We flew from the UK on 26 April 1996 and were met by Mark. We were soon immersed in Ospreys, hacking cages, visiting sites and discussing with his staff and volunteers the highs and lows of translocating young Osprey chicks. A full week was spent in Minneapolis and we all felt as we made our way back to the airport that the visit had been a huge success. We felt confident that when the time came for us we would have no problem carrying out similar procedures back in Rutland. Little did we know what waited for us on our return.

Mark Martell with a North American Osprey.

Once again Roy Dennis took the lead, dealing with the PHVA and sending his comments back to SNH on 8 May 1996. Time was marching on and if we were indeed to start the translocation that year then the window of opportunity was rapidly closing as we would need to collect chicks of the right age from their Scottish nests in less than two months' time.

Roy's letter dealt succinctly with all the points required by SNH, covering everything from the genetic health of the Scottish population to the collection areas, the age and size of chicks to be removed, the total number of chicks needed to create a viable breeding population, the long-term suitability of Rutland Water for Ospreys, the pros and cons of natural colonisation and future monitoring. In fact much of this detail was already in the application, just not in the form of a PHVA.

We kept ourselves busy while waiting for the outcome of our PHVA, taking a calculated risk that we would be granted a licence. Time was running out and if the licence was granted at the last moment we would need to have the temporary holding cages ready and waiting. Under the supervision of Senior Warden Martyn Aspinall, staff and volunteers started to construct two elevated holding pens, one on Brown's Island, the other on Lagoon 3.

Finally, on 11 June 1996 the long-awaited letter landed on my desk – together with a licence to collect 8–12 birds. The jubilation felt by all those involved is indescribable. At the same time we knew we had a massive task ahead and that the world of conservation would be scrutinising our every move; there were still some who felt that the whole project was a PR stunt led by the water company and the Trust. How wrong they were proved to be.

We realised there would be considerable interest from both national and local media when the translocated birds arrived and this certainly proved to be the case. However, our priority had to be the chicks – the sudden glare of a media frenzy was the last thing we wanted to expose them to. A carefully managed plan was agreed whereby one chick, the strongest, would be shown to the cameras in a specially built cage resembling the holding pens but well away from the actual pens themselves.

The big day eventually arrived, the press and invited guests gathered by the Burley Fishponds in the northern section of the reserve and in no time at all a vehicle appeared, carrying its precious cargo. The date was 10 July 1996, a day that will live with me for the rest of my life, as it began a journey that in years to come would bring so many people together from so many different backgrounds, counties, countries and even continents; a journey so unexpected on that warm, sunny day in Rutland.

An unringed Scottish female resting at Rutland Water during her autumn migration in 1997.

Volunteer Diary, Paul Stammers, 1996

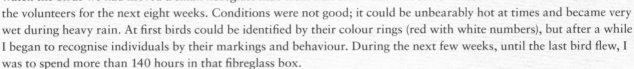

I can still remember my first meeting with Helen McIntyre – it was May 1996 and I was considering early retirement and looking for things to do with my spare time. I was asked whether I would like to volunteer with the Osprey team, and so my adventures with Ospreys began.

Other volunteers were assembled as part of the monitoring team too. We would watch the behaviour of the birds from the day they arrived until they set out on that first journey to West Africa. On 10 July 1996, seven young birds arrived from Scotland. The birds were soon settled and given their first feed of Rutland trout. We cut the trout into small pieces, then slowly slid each piece down a pipe into the nest. To enable us to watch the birds we had moved a small fibreglass hide from Lax Hill – this was to be home for the volunteers for the next eight weeks. Conditions were not good; it could be unbearably hot at times and became very wet during heavy rain. At first birds could be identified by their colour rings (red with white numbers), but after a while I began to recognise individuals by their markings and behaviour. During the next few weeks, until the last bird flew, I was to spend more than 140 hours in that fibreglass box.

The highlight of my first season came on 30 July, the day we released the first birds. I arrived at the hide at about 4.30am so I could get settled before the cage was opened. At 7am the front of the pen was slowly lowered, and the wait began. Roy Dennis had advised us that once the cage was opened we needed to minimise movement in front of the birds, as this might deter them from leaving the cage. So we waited and waited. Wings were stretched, wings were flapped but the birds did not seem to be ready to leave the security of their cage. I was willing birds 16 and 17 to make their first flights. Finally bird 16 lifted off the nest, hovered for a while and, at 2.26pm, left the safety of the pens for the first time. After a short flight 16 landed on one of the perches we'd erected between the hide and the release pens.

What a moment! I'd spent 12 hours in the cramped hide but it was worth it. I'd seen the first Rutland Osprey fledge.

Volunteer Diary, Mike Lewin, 2010

After a period of dull weather, Sunday 12 September dawned dry and sunny. It was a largely uneventful morning in Manton Bay. Much to everyone's surprise, three Ospreys had remained there long after Rutland's other Ospreys had departed. 5R(04), the adult male, was on his usual perch in front of Shallow Water Hide. His mate, the unringed female, had spent a short period alongside 5R(04) during the morning, but by midday he was on the perch by the nest site, close to the remaining juvenile 30(10). His incessant food-begging rang out across Manton Bay, but neither parent showed any inclination to fish. At 12.15pm, the unringed female left her perch and circled slowly, at low level, over the bay. For a while she held this position, then gradually she circled higher and higher, still directly above the nest site. After several minutes she was a very distant bird in the Rutland sky. Suddenly, as if locking on to the migration route, she burst into rapid flight and sped southwards, quickly disappearing from view. Her permanent presence in the bay since early April was over; her migration had begun.

The young Osprey had watched his mother's departure in silence, but now he turned his attention to 5R(04). He flew towards the adult male, loudly food-begging, but to no avail and soon he was back on his perch by the nest. There he sat silently, surveying the changed scene. How would he react to events? An hour passed, then the juvenile lifted off from his perch and like his mother before him slowly circled over the water. Gradually he flew higher, still circling, until he too was just a speck in the sky above Manton Bay. Then, it was the same fast, direct flight southwards. The young Osprey, hatched just 14 weeks earlier, was on his way to Africa with only instinct to guide him.

Now, as in late March, 5R(04) remained the only Osprey in Manton Bay. The season was ending as it had begun. Soon, in the wake of his family, he would be on his way and sadly, another Osprey summer at Rutland Water would be over. What a pleasure it has been to watch the Manton Bay Ospreys this summer and what a privilege to witness the departure of these magnificent birds on their migration. We wish them well and look forward to their safe return.

Translocation and Welcome Returns

PREPARATIONS

Roy and Tim had recently returned from their fact-finding trip to Minnesota with Mark Martell. There they had witnessed the delicate work of hand feeding the five-week-old Osprey chicks by a dedicated group of women at the 'hacking' site. It had been agreed that the Rutland Osprey Project should mirror the US project as closely as possible and to this end a female project officer was required. So began my involvement in this ground-breaking story. What was to have been on paper a simple task of a few weeks of 'animal husbandry' (albeit of the most privileged sort) soon evolved to a take on a much wider remit culminating in a completely absorbing and fascinating seven years with the project.

With the requisite licences in hand from both SNH and English Nature, we had the green light for the translocation to begin and just two weeks in which to prepare the release sites and put the logistics in place. Crucial to this phase was the work of the volunteer team under the leadership of Martyn Aspinall, the Senior Reserve Warden.

In 1996, two sites were carefully chosen to house the young birds for the critical pre-release phase. Both offered open views of the lagoons, but were in sheltered locations hidden away from public gaze and in areas closed to general access. Martyn's volunteer team set about constructing the pens. Based on the American model, each set was raised some 4.5 metres above the ground, accessible by a removable ladder and divided into two separate compartments, each

TOP Martyn Aspinall building the release pens on Lagoon 3.

BOTTOM The release site on Brown's Island.

Rutland Water Nature Reserve Senior Warden Martyn Aspinall and a team of volunteers attempting to catch fish for the translocated Ospreys.

measuring 1.8 by 1.2 metres. Within each of these a 1-metre artificial nest was created out of sticks and fresh hay, to closely resemble a natural eyrie. The back of each pen was solid, with an integral feeding hatch to allow the chicks to be fed with minimal disturbance.

Beside the elevated structure we erected several T-perches in readiness for the young birds' release. Further life-size artificial eyries had been constructed on telegraph poles around the reserve. These would serve not only as perching sites for the fledglings, but also as potential future nesting sites. A small garden shed acted as the monitoring hut from where, via CCTV, the minutiae of each chick's daylight hours could be recorded.

At Fishponds Cottage, the transformation of a former stable to a state-of-the-art whitewashed 'fish room' was under way. This was later to become Osprey HQ and was the scene of many hours of rewriting the rule book during those early years.

Martyn's team became experts in the art of laying fyke nets (bag-shaped fishing nets held open by hoops) in the lagoons on the reserve as work began to stock the freezer with a variety of locally caught fish. Once a week, a six-man crew set out with a seine net to catch pike, Perch, Roach and eel from the main body of the reservoir. The art of gutting these coarse fish was a necessary but new skill to me.

Helen McIntyre preparing the fish caught by Martyn and his team. When the translocated birds first arrived fish was cut into small, fingernail-sized pieces. As they became more adept at feeding, larger pieces were introduced.

COLLECTION

On 12 July 1996 I set out from Rutland Water in an Anglian Water transit van on the 450-mile journey north to Inverness-shire. It was a drive that I was to make many times over the next five years, but on that day it heralded the beginning of a fascinating adventure.

Driving into Boat of Garten, it became apparent that the Osprey was big business – the fish-hawk logo was ubiquitous on B&B signs, information centres and cafes. However, as I crossed the Spey and left the village, I had a growing sense of the remoteness of the pine forests and glens with which the Osprey had become synonymous over the past 50 years.

Roy Dennis's croft in Nethybridge is in an open area of undulating cattle-grazed meadows, just beyond the bounds of the famous Loch Garten bird reserve. Here, in amongst the birches, Roy had erected a row of holding pens, used to house Red Kites for a previous translocation project.

During the course of the next four days, Roy and a number of helpers collected seven chicks from nests on private estates. Potential donor nests had been identified during the course of his spring survey and a shortlist of accessible nests had been drawn up. When contacted, all the landowners had responded with great enthusiasm and interest and some even helped with the collection visits. Eyrie trees were climbed using ladders and ropes, and the whole brood was lowered to the ground in a canvas bag. Once on the ground each chick was checked for condition

Boat of Garten – the home of Ospreys in Scotland.

Collecting chicks for the translocation.

Roy Dennis assessing potential chicks for translocation.

Roy Dennis and colleague collecting chicks on Forestry Commission land.

before being weighed, measured and ringed with a metal BTO ring together with a coloured PVC lettered ring, known as a Darvic. The chick destined for England was ringed on the opposite leg to its siblings, which were then returned carefully to the nest. The parents, which had been circling overhead, quickly settled back to their normal duties within moments of the team leaving.

In that first year, perhaps mindful of the project's detractors and under some pressure from SNH, it was agreed to remove the smallest chick from nests of three. This, together with the challenging task of taking the young during the slimmest of pre-fledging windows, greatly limited the number of nest sites available. These were sited over a large geographical spread in the Highland and Moray study areas, and the collection of the five- to six-week-old donor birds during that first year was an exhausting and at times demoralising task.

Back at Roy's home near Nethybridge, I began the job of feeding the young chicks three times a day on locally procured trout. Initially we simply left small, finger-sized pieces on little wooden boards at the edge of the nest in the hope that the birds would help themselves. Such an approach was very low-key in comparison with the methods used in Minnesota, where a gloved hand puppet was used to entice the young chicks to feed. In our view such disguises were unnecessary as Ospreys are unlikely to imprint. However, through careful monitoring, it did become clear that some of the birds were simply too young and would need hand feeding. This was a lengthy and at times frustrating process requiring a great deal of patience on my part and trust and acceptance on the part of the chicks.

On 15 July 1996, with our complement of seven chicks and a rendezvous with the press the following morning, Roy and I made hasty preparations for our departure that evening. We had decided to make the nine-hour journey at night, when conditions were cooler and the birds would naturally be resting. However, a serious complication arose when the Anglian Water van failed to start. It appeared to be completely immobilised. Our remote location and 'out of hours' situation made a repair out of the question and there was no question of delaying the press conference. We had to make the journey that night. The solution came by way of a speedy and luxurious journey in Roy's BMW, all chicks stowed in their cardboard boxes as rear-seat passengers, arriving safely to a greeting by an enthusiastic press the following morning. An eighth chick was brought down separately by Roy on 27 July.

Two juveniles in the release pens shortly after their arrival in July 1996. The chicks were translocated at around six weeks of age.

The first Ospreys were greeted by the press when they arrived at Rutland Water in 1996 – a historic day for the project and for Osprey conservation in the UK.

BACK AT RUTLAND

At the outset, we'd been very clear, both in our own minds and publicly, that the first year of the project was to be regarded as an experimental one. After all, Osprey translocations had not been attempted outside the USA and as such this was a pioneering project for Europe. We had undoubtedly anticipated some teething problems, but little had we appreciated what a steep learning curve lay before us. As it was the lessons learnt during the subsequent pre-release phase proved to be incredibly valuable and shaped the project in the years to come.

With the chicks installed in mixed aged broods at the two sites we began to monitor their daily food intake and activity. Despite the invaluable 'fly-on-the-wall' view provided by the CCTV cameras we quickly realised that identifying each individual by its ring number alone was rarely possible and that we would need to familiarise ourselves with each distinctive and individual head pattern. In later years, when colour cameras were installed, we overcame this problem by colour-spotting each bird in various colour and number combinations.

In those early weeks every wing flap, stretch, scratch and bowel movement was recorded. Through the detailing of such minutiae we were able to build up a picture of each individual bird's development, health and progress. Of course over time we realised that we were witnessing a normal pattern of increasing activity and interest in the outside world, but in those early weeks, rather like new parents watching their firstborn, each new move held its own fascination and excitement.

During the first year, the importance of the detailed monitoring and recording became apparent when two of the birds at the Lagoon 3 site, one a runt that had been rescued at four weeks of age, began to show worrying signs of inactivity and poor health. With their plumage beginning to take on a lacklustre appearance, a decrease in appetite and an apparent inability to defecate out of the nest (normally Ospreys are meticulous housekeepers) our concern was such that we asked Dr James Kirkwood from the Institute of Zoology and a renowned expert on raptors to visit the project.

Following the subsequent death of one of these birds at the Lagoon 3 site, Dr Kirkwood made a further visit to examine two birds in particular, whose condition appeared to be deteriorating, and to take blood samples. One was later moved to a specially prepared aviary at Fishponds Cottage for closer monitoring. With such precious individuals these were extremely worrying times for us and every effort was made to revive the failing chicks. Sadly, despite assiduous medical care, one chick failed to revive and had to be euthanised at the Institute of Zoology in London.

Following a post-mortem, a detailed report by Dr Kirkwood concluded that a salmonella infection had been a contributory factor in the loss of four of our eight chicks during that first year. The source of the infection was not clear; perhaps it had come from wild birds at the artificial nests or via the food. It was also possible that one of the chicks was a carrier at the time of translocation. An examination of the history of the donor nests revealed unexplained problems with one eyrie in particular, which

Translocated juveniles in the Lax Hill release pens. The pens were relocated there from Lagoon 3 and Brown's Island in 1997 as the site's more open, elevated location presented fewer hazards for the young birds during their first few days on the wing.

had seen a higher than expected number of dead young over the years, including some unusual defects. No further chicks were taken from this nest in later years.

This episode marked a serious low point for the team. During those first few weeks the work with the chicks had been not only physically intense and exhausting but also emotionally absorbing. Unlike other raptor translocation projects, notably those for the Red Kites and White-tailed Eagles, we had the advantage of working with a species that couldn't be imprinted. Nevertheless, these were wild birds and our aim was to minimise human contact and handling wherever possible. However, as their principal feeder and carer in those very early days I quickly learnt that each chick had its own character and charming idiosyncrasies. When hand feeding, for example, Roy had suggested that I talk to the birds so they might become familiar with the sound of my voice and manner. The threatened, aggressive high-pitched alarm squeals that greeted me as I entered the pens quickly changed to appreciative whistles, once the chicks had accepted the food and wanted more.

The identification of infection led to some key changes in the project following the losses in that experimental first year. Foremost was the decision to only take healthy, strong donor birds in future. Rather than being able to 'save' the youngest runt bird, it was clear to us that the natural parents were much better equipped to raise a healthy brood once one of the stronger chicks had been removed. SNH accepted this and our licence for 1997 was redrawn accordingly, together with a clause allowing a certain number of chicks to be taken from nests of two young rather than just broods of three. With the Forestry Commission enthusiastically offering chicks from nests on their estates we were able to widen our choice of eyries. Unfortunately in 1997 a cold, damp June turned into an unseasonably wet July, leading to the failure of many broods. Despite this Roy managed to collect a further eight chicks. Between 1998 and 2001, however, a full complement of 12 young was collected and translocated each year, bringing the total to 64 young over six years.

A further change lay in the age at which chicks were taken. In Minnesota donor chicks were taken from the nest at five weeks. Although it's difficult to be certain, we believe the eight translocated in the 1996 season ranged from just 30 days old (this being the rescued runt) to 40 days. With the inherent difficulties of hand feeding and the health problems we encountered that year we decided in future years to increase the collection age to 6–6½ weeks, determined by a minimum wing length of 320mm. By this time the birds would largely be self-feeding and past the critical period of bone growth and quill development. This change proved to be of enormous benefit and no further birds were lost at this pre-release stage in subsequent years.

READY FOR FREEDOM

As the weeks passed, an observable change in the chicks' behaviour was detected, with the older birds in each pen beginning to take a keener interest in the world beyond the netting. Rather than spending time in the body of the nest they favoured the stumps and perches located at the front of each pen, passing the hours in watchful silence. From time to time personnel involved in the project passed in front of the pens, to accustom the chicks to the sight of humans; the English Midlands are a far cry from the remote wilds of Scotland and if this pioneering Osprey 'population' was to succeed they could not be deterred by dog walkers, fishermen or cyclists. It seemed initially they were less comfortable with the sight of passing planes, vehicles and even other birds. Such disturbances were met by a threatened response, with the chicks falling prone in the nest bed, playing dead. However, as they became more used to their surroundings such reactions were less frequent and a cocking of the head or 'head bobbing' was the more typical response.

RELEASED AT LAST

Over the years we came to recognise when the young Ospreys were ready to be released. Activity levels increased, with manic bouts of wing flapping leading to 'helicoptering' and eventually short hops from perch to perch. At the same time, they became much more wary of human intervention, reacting to the point of aggression on the rare occasions that the pens were entered. Few of the team who entered the pens escaped without the scars to show for it – it left us in no doubt that these were indeed wild birds and that no imprinting had taken place. Litter-picking forceps were eventually used to remove the uneaten fish parts from the pens.

Overall the translocated birds fledged slightly later than their 'wild' counterparts so as to ensure their optimum condition for release. Releasing them was a major gamble and we had to be convinced that the birds were fit and strong enough to fend for themselves. Although the Minnesota experience gave us confidence, we had no idea whether 'our birds' would consider the pens as home and return to them once they'd experienced freedom.

Before release Dr Kirkwood, and latterly his colleague Sue Thornton from the International Zoo Veterinary Group, gave each bird a health check. This involved taking the birds in turn from the pens, covering their heads with a towel or falconer's hood to keep them still and calm, and carefully checking them over before taking several small blood samples from them for DNA analysis (and to confirm their sex, which had been determined by us with a satisfying 100% accuracy using a rather arbitrary method of a combination of size and ankle width – the slimmer ankles for the males and wider for the females) and routine haematological screening. Following our concerns in the first year faecal samples were taken from each pen and tested for parasites and worms. However, by 2000 it became clear that these were no longer necessary as no significant abnormalities had been detected since our techniques for caring for the birds had been refined in 1997.

At the same time we weighed each bird using a pair of old kitchen scales, and measured its wing and tail feathers. We carefully checked the feathers to make sure they were hard penned, indicating that they were fully developed and ready for flight.

The final procedure was to fit the radio-tracking transmitter. This would allow us to follow the birds both immediately following release and later as they explored the wider area before migration. Each transmitter was carefully fitted to the shaft of the central tail feather using a clever combination of plastic tubing, dental floss and superglue. Each was given a unique numerical code and when all were found to be in working order the chicks were returned to the pens.

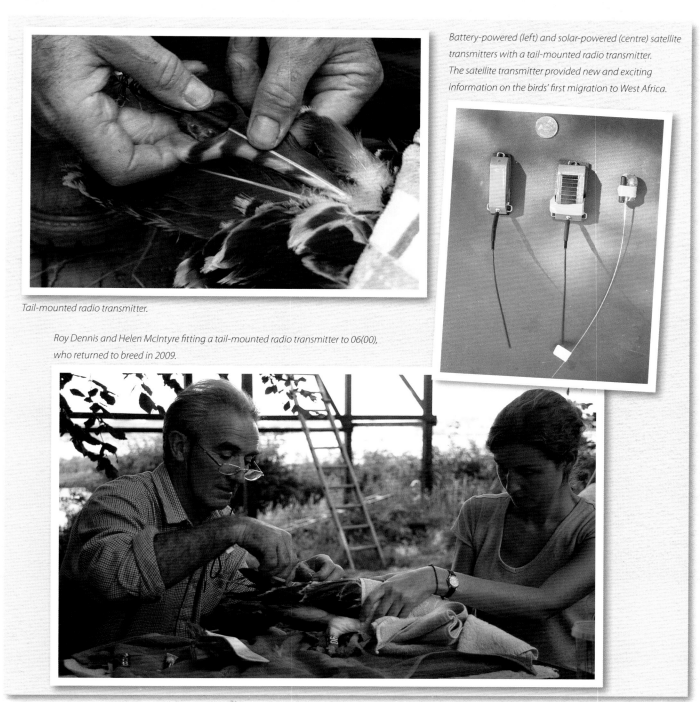

Battery-powered (left) and solar-powered (centre) satellite transmitters with a tail-mounted radio transmitter. The satellite transmitter provided new and exciting information on the birds' first migration to West Africa.

Tail-mounted radio transmitter.

Roy Dennis and Helen McIntyre fitting a tail-mounted radio transmitter to 06(00), who returned to breed in 2009.

Release day in 2000. The fronts of the pens were slowly lowered using baler twine, so as not to flush the juveniles. Some birds would remain on the edges of the pens for several hours before taking their first flight.

Once the birds had received the veterinary all-clear we were able to group them according to their readiness for release, and we put all the older birds together in the same pen. The final criterion on our list was clear fine weather – rain with low pressure was sure to dampen their enthusiasm for flight.

On 30 July 1996, with volunteers and reserve staff positioned at strategic locations around the reserve and communicating via two-way radios, we carefully opened the first of the pens holding the most advanced birds. Our approach differed from that for the Red Kites, which due to quarantine regulations had been held far beyond their natural fledging age, and were cajoled noisily from their holding pens with bangs and whoops in front of an invited crowd. In this case, so as not to disturb the Ospreys, we lowered the fronts of the release pens inch by inch from below using a 'Heath Robinson' system involving lengths of baler twine.

As the fronts came down and were secured in place they created a small platform, allowing the fledglings to take to the air in their own time. Having no idea how the birds would react, yet anticipating an immediate bid for freedom, this was a heart-stopping and thrilling moment. That first year, however, the birds were slow and cautious, sometimes taking several hours to make their maiden flights. One didn't fly at all for about 48 hours after it was first released; the front of the pen was later closed and the bird was released for a second time two days later. Of the six young to be released that first year, only one bird took off without warning. For the rest, a tentative edging onto the mesh preceded each flight. Once the ground beneath the meshing or over the edge of the platform became visible, there was some vigorous head bobbing and usually a sudden flurry of activity before the flight. Watching each year's cohort of birds take to the air was always unpredictable and nerve-racking, but also incredibly exciting, and release day became a highlight of the translocation season.

Recently released juveniles on the artificial nest on Lax Hill, known as AN1.

ON THE WING

The days that followed the release of the '1996 six' taught us a great deal about the hazards facing newly fledged Ospreys and above all the importance of location in siting the release pens in future years. It also underlined how important it was to closely monitor the inexperienced birds, particularly by radio tracking. While a number of the early flights were 'textbook', with a short and localised flight coming to a rather shaky end on an artificial nest, others gave us more cause for concern. Several birds had to be recovered from areas of dense scrub or reedy vegetation, and rehoused overnight before being re-released the following day. Sadly one was not so lucky, its inexperience apparently leading to its demise – it was found drowned having apparently alighted on and then fallen through a dense patch of algae at the water's edge.

Another bird, having been disturbed by passing sheep, alighted in the leafy branches of a very tall willow tree, from which it struggled to extricate itself. As the hours passed and its attempts to fly became more frantic a decision was taken to climb the tree in order to flush the reluctant bird. This too failed and the bird was left to roost in situ overnight. It remained in the tree for a further 19 hours before taking to the wing, apparently unharmed.

Such experiences were indeed salutary. The overly sheltered and windless south-facing Lagoon 3 site was abandoned and recommendations were made to strim the vegetation immediately around the Brown's Island release pens. We further planned to create more natural perching sites by ring barking the mature trees, and to erect additional artificial perches. However, before the 1997 season, the decision was made to abandon these low-lying release sites in favour of the elevated, mature and mixed deciduous woodland at Lax Hill. With its favourable updraughts and its plentiful mature and decaying or dead trees it provided a perfect fledging, perching and roosting site for the young Ospreys, and the copse had been frequented by the juveniles the previous year. A new, much larger release site was constructed on the shady north side of the wood, fronted by a large area of close-cropped open grassland and overlooking the lagoons, the open water of the reservoir and woodland beyond.

With the new site up and running, together with our agreement with the licensing authorities to collect stronger and older cohorts of birds, the project entered a new and positive phase. With the terrible losses we encountered during the 1996 season now behind us we were able to raise, release and see to migration 55 of the 56 birds translocated between 1997 and 2001, the single loss being attributable to a newly fledged bird seemingly flying into a power line on a neighbouring estate.

The release pens on Lax Hill. The birds were kept in the pens for between two and three weeks in groups of three, to replicate the usual brood size.

Juvenile Osprey perched on Hambleton church spire after a long first flight in 1998.

top of the church steeple in Hambleton village. The fledgling remained on the peninsula for the next 24 hours, spending much of this time on a chimney on the roof of the exclusive Hambleton Hall Hotel, until returning to the release site.

Again and again we were reminded of the importance of close monitoring and keeping an accurate record of the fledglings' progress. In the early post-release phase a lengthy absence would start to ring alarm bells. Invariably our concerns were justified and search teams were sent out to pinpoint radio signals deep within scrub or reeds. In Minnesota, where no such radio tracking was used, a bird that didn't return to the hack site in the days following release was assumed, quite mistakenly as it turned out, to have migrated or to be foraging elsewhere. Levels of mortality at this stage in wild populations are not known, but if comparisons with other raptors, such as Buzzards, can be made, they are thought to be in the order of 10%.

From 1997 onwards all post-release monitoring took place from 'the outpost', an ineptly camouflaged 1960s caravan that had seen the Reserve Manager's family through many a holiday in his youth. Now, sited against a sheltered hedge line at the foot of Lax Hill, it became the focal point for note taking, radio communication and Osprey gossip. To complement the visual monitoring, using binoculars and telescopes to identify birds by ring number or markings, two radio-tracking devices were purchased and over the years the staff and volunteers of the project team became experts in the art of the 'yagi'. With a large three-point metal aerial held aloft, connected to a weighty metal box, this often raised eyebrows when encountered by the public off the reserve.

This isn't to say that we didn't have our anxious moments. On one very memorable occasion in 1998, one of our regular volunteers, a vicar at a local church, was present at an early-morning watch to monitor the release of one chick. As the bird took to the air it was unwittingly carried by strong south-westerly winds across the open reservoir in the direction of the Hambleton Peninsula. At volunteer changeover time the vicar left his post with a promise to pray for the bird's safe return. Several nail-biting hours followed and it was with great relief that as the light began to fade the bird was spotted on

The late Eric Locker and Lawrence Martyn monitoring the translocated juveniles from the outpost. The translocated birds were monitored closely by a team of staff and volunteers from the day they arrived from Scotland, until their departure in early September.

The juveniles were fitted with tail-mounted radio transmitters, allowing us to monitor their daily flights using tracking equipment, known as a yagi. This proved especially useful during the young birds' first few days on the wing, when some crash-landed in thick vegetation.

Using this two-tier system of aural and visual identification, we were able to build up a picture of each bird's movements during the weeks after its release. Initially, flights tended to be short and localised between perches but, over time and with growing confidence, their length, duration and range increased. The month or so after fledging and before migration is known to be crucial in allowing the birds to familiarise themselves with the lie of the land and the map of the stars, thus imprinting this landscape of 'home' on their memories and allowing them to navigate back to Rutland on their first return migration.

In our attempts to keep track we expanded the monitoring team to five separate locations, but even with this coverage it became more difficult to locate the birds. Each year we liaised with English Nature personnel working on the East Midlands Red Kite project near Corby, swapping the unique numbers of our respective birds in order to widen our area of field. When successful, our searches revealed that the young regularly used neighbouring estates and remote valleys further afield for perching, and occasionally roosting at night. However, such attempts were often fruitless and we had to resign ourselves to waiting for the evening feeds. These became critical for 'counting in' the birds and it was always a relief to know that the day had ended with a full complement of young.

The juveniles were not always alone in flight and provided endless entertainment for the local populations of Jackdaws and Carrion Crows, which each year had to share their territory with the interlopers. Other raptors were seen to vie for air space with the young birds; once a juvenile male Peregrine Falcon was seen attempting to snatch a fish from an Osprey's grip. Kestrel, Red Kite, Sparrowhawk, Buzzard and Marsh Harrier were also recorded interacting with the young.

While the released young were persistent in their endeavours to catch fish, few were seen to be successful. With plentiful supplies of food back at base this was never a problem while the young remained at Rutland Water. However, in no more than a matter of days or weeks, the young inexperienced fishermen would be reliant on their unhoned skills for providing the energy to fuel their long migrations. This thought didn't fill us with optimism.

We continued to provide food for the birds throughout their post-release period, just as the male parent bird does in the wild. Initially we placed fish on the artificial nests on Brown's Island using a rudimentary system comprising a cut-away plastic lemonade bottle taped to a 5 metre-long pole. In subsequent years we climbed a ladder to place the fish on wooden feeding boxes erected on poles in the open field in front of the release pens. After a while the birds abandoned these feeding stations in favour of the roof of the release pens. Again this required some ingenuity both in order to maintain some degree of hygiene and also to minimise disturbance to the birds, which were easily flushed. A solution was found in simply placing the fish on top of crates filled with woodchips (which could be changed at regular intervals to avoid contamination); these were then pushed to the fronts of the release pens on wooden runners using a hooked pole.

Fish supply was carefully monitored to reflect consumption, and a daily order of fresh trout was placed with a local fish farm. The hesitancy that came with the first few days of freedom soon gave way to a settled pattern of feeding. Again in time and with experience, we learnt that our idea of early-morning feeds was simply not early enough for the birds, which started food-begging at first light. We therefore gave them a daily feed every afternoon, with sufficient supplies to cover the following morning's meal. The timing of the afternoon feed tended to be set by the birds themselves. This was adapted according to both the weather (hot days requiring a later evening feed, for example) and the amount of daylight, with the time being brought forward as the season progressed.

Typically the birds would come looking for food, settling in the familiar perches on Lax Hill. Some were persistent food-beggers, calling with a loud, rasping 'quee-quee-quee' in their eagerness to be fed. Often the younger birds would be observed food-begging from the older ones and on occasions were seen snatching food from the unwary. As in the nest, hierarchies developed, with younger subordinate birds 'waiting in turn' until their more dominant peers moved away. Birds often carried fish from a feeding station to a perch, with the current favourite reflecting their expanding territories.

In August 1999 returning sub-adults were seen taking advantage of the 'easy pickings' provided at the food stations. This coincidentally followed a period of heavy rain that may have made fishing difficult in the open water. The following year a 1998-released bird became a frequent visitor at feeding time, prompting the newly released young to food-beg incessantly.

Lawrence Ball and Jamie Weston netting fish for the translocated juveniles at a local fish farm. One of the advantages the translocated birds had over juveniles at natural nests was that they could be guaranteed a constant supply of food.

Tim Mackrill putting fish on the feed trays on the Lax Hill release pens in 2000. The birds were fed in this way twice a day.

Juvenile, with satellite transmitter, on the Lax Hill feed trays in 1999.

Juveniles feeding on the Lax Hill feed trays.

TIME TO GO

The 'empty-nest syndrome' was never more apt than for those of us who saw the four birds of the first cohort in 1996 from fledging through to migration. The previous eight weeks had been an intensive and at times emotional journey of highs and lows and suddenly, as the yagi fell silent for the last time on 9 September, it was all over.

The migration data gathered during the translocation phase of the project were found to be largely consistent with those of both Scotland and Minnesota. On average the birds were about 12 weeks old, setting out towards the end of August (earliest date 22 August) through to mid-September (last recorded 21 September). Our records showed that wind directions were highly variable, coming from the north, west or south but never from the east. Climatic triggers appeared to have influenced the timing of departure, with the first cold night of the year often acting as the spur and migration only taking place under high-pressure conditions with broken or sunny skies. Although Ospreys migrate singly it was not uncommon for a number to leave on the same day. In 2001, for example, following days of overcast skies and rain, six birds migrated on 27 August. It was clear that if conditions were not right the birds would simply stay put. Even now, despite the passage of time, come a breezy, sunny September day I often find myself thinking how perfect it would be for migration.

TRACKING GOES GLOBAL

In 1996, without the aid of satellite-tracking equipment and despite our best efforts to alert the general public and birdwatchers to the possibility of sighting the juveniles, our expectations for identifying and locating the birds, either on passage or in their overwintering grounds, were very low. On 14 September a Rutland juvenile was recorded eating a fish at Pilsey Sands near Chichester, Sussex, having been identified as one of the translocated young by a red Darvic ring on its left leg (Scottish young that year carried a similar red ring on their right legs).

Over the subsequent years we received a very limited number of sightings or ring recoveries of non-satellite tagged birds. Each year up to 25 local bird clubs in the UK were sent the list of ring numbers, as were several abroad, including the Tanji Birding Club of The Gambia and the Gibraltar Ornithological and Natural History Society (GOHNS). The search for the Rutland young even went airborne when the RAF became involved. In 1998 personnel manning the radios

Translocated juveniles at Rutland Water before migration.

on Gibraltar scanned for Rutland birds over a number of months using equipment that had been specially brought in for the exercise, but without success.

Building on these early links, in September 1998 the Project Assistant, Tricia Galpin, and I had a fascinating visit to Gibraltar and Andalucía to investigate the potential for tracking the translocated juveniles on migration. During our visit we met representatives from the GONHS and the Birdlife partner in Spain, SEO. The latter mounts a three-month raptor watch each year as part of the MIGRES programme, funded in part by the EU. Monitoring points have been established along the coastline between Algeciras and Tarifa, with volunteers at 12 stations maintaining radio links with the team at the long-standing project on Gibraltar. The sight of thousands of raptors passing overhead is an incredible and memorable spectacle. However, the proportion of Osprey sightings was distinctly low compared with other species. It had long been suspected that Ospreys are less inclined to rely on the thermals generated at this point in the Mediterranean, preferring to migrate across on a much broader band. The advent of our linked satellite-tracking programmes, described later, certainly confirmed this.

In July 1997 Roy Dennis received news of a ring recovery of bird 16 (translocated in 1996) in an area south of Dakar, Senegal, in February that year. Unfortunately details were very scant, but we were heartened in this early stage of the project to know that the translocated young were clearly resident in the normal wintering grounds of Scottish Ospreys.

A further and rather heart-warming tale reached us of Osprey 04(01), which left Rutland Water on 4 September

1997 and was found dying in a field near Conakry, Guinea, on 4 August 1998. An impoverished farmer, Mr Abdoura Hamane Compo, had caught the exhausted and injured bird in his fields and took it home, when at '20:00 hours its soul went to heaven'. As he was preparing it for the pot he noticed the rings on its legs and, in his words, 'knew it to be on a mission'. There followed a string of rather sad occurrences. Having decided to seek help at the town hall Mr Compo fell ill. When he'd recovered three days later he decided to take a ride to the town, but there were no vehicles so he was forced to cycle. Having met a Canadian living locally, who explained the significance of his now rather pungent find, he cut off the bird's legs to remove the rings. With the important details contained on the rings he continued to the capital and passed by the British Embassy, where he was turned away by the commissionaire. Finally, with the help of a translator and scribe, a letter was penned and forwarded to the BTO giving us the fascinating details.

With the advent of satellite tracking our knowledge of Osprey migration has been transformed, and as a result of the tracking of Scottish, English and latterly Welsh Ospreys some of the mysteries of migration have now been solved. There can be no denying, however, that in the first three years of the project we had no idea whether we would see any of the Ospreys again or whether the project stood any chance of success. But this all changed in May 1999, with the return of the first of the Rutland young.

Roy Dennis painting two decoy Ospreys in preparation for siting them on Brown's Island. The models were intended to attract Ospreys to the artificial nests, but they only succeeded in attracting unwanted attention from crows. This technique has, however, been used successfully in Corsica.

A MILESTONE

Each year, before the first sighting of any Ospreys in the UK, all the artificial nests on the reserve were refurbished by volunteer tree surgeon Linsay Brown, who generously gave his time to ensure the nests were in peak condition and inviting to any passing or returning Osprey. Each year, the Manton Bay nest proved to be too tempting for a pair of Canada Geese, which took up residence early each spring, giving any returning birds the unwelcome job of displacing them.

In 1999 the nest-refurbishment task took on a particular significance, being the first year in which we might expect our juveniles, now sub-adults of pre-breeding age, to return. As an additional enticement Roy arrived with two polystyrene decoy Ospreys that were secured to the artificial nest and perch on Brown's Island. With a lick of dark brown and white paint these made a convincing pair.

Decoy Ospreys have been used with great success in Corsica, where competition for existing nest sites was such that the population had stopped increasing. By placing decoys on and beside artificial nests in different parts of the island new colonies have been formed and the population has had room to grow. One of the Rutland decoys was an original from Corsica and even bore the scars of attacks by 'intruders'. Over several weeks the pair suffered further damage and the decoys were finally taken down, having been partially destroyed by resident Carrion Crows who found sport in repeatedly attacking them.

FIRST RETURN

It was a remarkable and unforgettable moment, seeing 08(97) perched in Manton Bay on 29 May 1999. Earlier in the afternoon, Tim Appleton had identified the male and immediately phoned in great excitement. This was the first sighting of the bird since its migration some 20 months previously on 4 September 1997. The significance of this moment cannot be overestimated. Here, after more than four years of hard work, expectation and hope, was the living proof that Rutland-raised chicks regarded this as home and our first real evidence that the project might succeed. 08(97) went on to become an iconic bird; doomed to be an inveterate bachelor until finally pairing successfully with 5N(04) in 2007. He went on to raise six chicks, before disappearing from his nest near the reservoir in suspicious circumstances in 2011.

Two weeks after 08(97)'s return on 14 June a sighting of an Osprey at a private estate some 8 miles from Rutland Water led us to believe that in fact two, rather than one, white-ringed juveniles had returned to the region. Both the local gamekeeper and Ian Carter from English Nature had seen the bird and contacted us. We were then able to confirm that this was in fact 03(97), which had also been released as a juvenile at Rutland Water on 27 July 1997 and was last seen on 4 September that year.

Both birds appeared to be in excellent condition and for the following three months were sighted regularly either at or near Rutland Water. Their presence at Rutland Water became more frequent during August, coinciding with the release of the juveniles on the reserve when almost daily sightings were recorded.

With the return from Africa of these two sub-adults the project entered a new phase. Although further translocations continued for the following two years these were by now fairly routine and by September 1999 the project had seen 36 young successfully released at Rutland Water, with 34 of them setting off on migration.

The following spring we eagerly watched the skies in anticipation of the safe return of 03(97) and 08(97). With both now of potential breeding age our expectations were (perhaps unrealistically) raised. However, we had to remember that their finding a mate was dependent on attracting a passing female. With the understanding that male Ospreys remain faithful to their natal site, and in line with the work undertaken in Minnesota, the Rutland project had biased selection of donor birds heavily in favour of males. In fact, by the end of its first five years, of the 52 birds reared 38 were confirmed as being male (through DNA testing) and ten female; the four birds that migrated in 1996 were not DNA tested but were thought to be two males and two females. Therefore in the unlikely event of a Rutland-released female returning and staying in the area that year the resident males would need to attract passage Scottish or Scandinavian females.

To this end, from his return on 16 April 2000, we witnessed concerted efforts by 03(97) to claim a territory centred around Lax Hill, with frequent carrying of sticks to the nest and much calling and displaying. He was joined on 24 April in the skies above the wood, and later displaced, by the second male, 08(97). During the summer months we were offered snapshots of potential pair bonding. From 20 May until 21 August a metal-ringed female was seen frequently with 08(97) in Manton Bay, and they were twice seen mating. Other reports told of ritualistic displays with the male bird flying high and dropping a stick into the water. The female then retrieved this and the roles were reversed. This was repeated six or seven times on at least three separate occasions.

In 2000 two new sub-adult birds, reared and released in 1998, returned to the locality, bringing the total number of returns to four. Perhaps we were witnessing the very beginnings of a new colony? During that summer we received

can appear very dark →

♂ 08(97) sitting in South Arm 2! First osprey to return from release program. 29.5.99

reports of a pair being sighted on a number of private estates in the area. In hindsight these proved to be highly significant.

What was to unfold became, over the course of the next few years, Rutland's most exciting but worst-kept secret. Time and time again we had witnessed 03(97) carrying sticks into what seemed a large area of woodland neighbouring the reservoir. Despite our attempts to pinpoint his destination through endless scanning of the horizon, we were unable to draw any conclusions. Our daily diary for that year notes that our first foray into the woodland on 7 May proved fruitless. Several others followed until we had traversed the woodland thoroughly from one side to another, without even a hint of Osprey activity. At last one day in late May Tim Appleton stepped out of the woodland, scanning the landscape before him and there, in a stag-headed oak, lay an eyrie of such dimensions that it seemed impossible to miss.

The location of the nest, which we began referring to as 'Site B', was perfect. Set some 20 metres high in the tree on an area of land well above the reservoir, it afforded fantastic 360-degree views of the surrounding fields, ponds, open water and the landscape far beyond the county boundary. To the left a dead tree would provide a perfect 'off-duty' perching site together with the stag-headed branches of the nest tree. Directly below and in front was a large open field, perfect for fledging. To the rear was a small copse, which screened the nest from a quiet country lane, the only public right of way in the area. With the landowner's enthusiastic consent we kept a gentle eye on the nest for the rest of the summer, eagerly awaiting the return of the Ospreys the following spring.

In 2001 the early arrivals of the two four-year-old males at their established territories signalled their clear intent to breed. 03(97) was the first to return on 28 March, some 19 days earlier than the previous year. On 3 April, to our growing excitement, an unringed female was seen with him at the Site B nest. However, her stay was brief and on 13 and 14 April, the same female was observed copulating with 08(97) on the nest platform in Manton Bay. The following day the male was again seen to mount the female, but by evening she had returned to Site B.

It seemed her mind had been made up. In response to her food-begging, 03(97) returned to the nest site with a fish and presented it to her. Such characteristic courtship feeding continued throughout the season. They were first seen mating on 18 April and by the end of the month it became evident that the incubation period had begun.

With the landowner's consent a small shed was erected among trees some 300 metres or so from the nest so we could keep a watchful eye on the breeding pair. Over the years the Site B nest has seen thousands of hours of Osprey activity recorded in logbooks by volunteers.

Of course the breeding behaviour of Ospreys in the wild has been well documented but, as with the early experimental years of the translocation, for the most part we were witnessing every detail with fresh eyes. We were in a new and exciting phase of the project and full of hope and expectation. A successful outcome might mean the very beginning of our Rutland colony.

To this end, we recorded every changeover, every stick brought to the nest, the type of fish and the comings and goings of any intruder Ospreys. As expected, the female was responsible for the majority of the incubation, only leaving the nest in order to feed on fish provided by the male. This pattern remained unchanged as the weeks passed into

Checking the Site B nest for recently hatched young using a mirror on the end of a long pole.

03(97) and his mate, perched beside the Site B nest having just arrived back from migration in 2001. Breeding Ospreys usually remain faithful to the same nest site and mate each year, but do not see their partner during the winter.

summer. Then on 6 June it seemed that a subtle change had occurred. Could it be that she was actually presenting tiny scraps of food deep into the bowl of the nest?

Confirmation came two days later when Roy Dennis and Tim Appleton visited the nest. Using a combination of a long pole with a mirror attached and binoculars they were able to confirm the presence of one chick and two eggs. By the time the chick could be seen in the nest ten days later, it was clear that the other two eggs had failed. When we later accessed the nest to ring the chick we could only find one egg. Could it be that the third egg had simply become buried in the nest lining (as the nest was built up to provide a level platform for the surviving chick, or had it indeed hatched and failed to survive? Unfortunately we would never know.

It was a historic moment when Tim Appleton secured the red Darvic ring number 13 to the chick's right leg on 14 July – the first Osprey chick to be reared in the English Midlands for at least 150 years and the first ever to be ringed. 13(01)'s size and measurements confirmed the bird to be female so when she set out on migration on 30 August, some 54 days after fledging, we knew that we were unlikely to see her in Rutland again. Indeed, there have been no sightings of her since 2001 and her fate is unknown, but, together with a single male reared at Bassenthwaite Lake in Cumbria that same season, her fledging marked a turning point for the species across England.

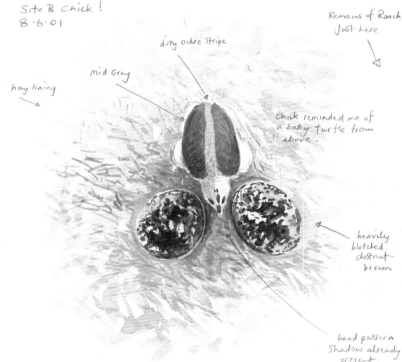

Site B chick !
8·6·01

Remains of Roach
just here

dirty ochre stripe

mid grey

hay lining

chick reminded me of a baby turtle from above.

heavily blotched chestnut-brown

head pattern shadow already present.

The chick hatched on about the 6th June. The 2nd egg may hatch today and the 3rd on 10th.
Roy Dennis came down from Scotland with extendable poles and a mirror to check contents of nest. We arrived at the nest at 09.10 hr and both adults circled high above, calling. No aggression from either of them though.
It took 10 poles to reach above the nest (about 55ft) and the above sketch is what we saw in the mirror !
Unbelievable sight and one I will never forget

Using a cherry picker to access the Site B nest.

13(01) in the nest before ringing.

13(01) being weighed.

13(01) before ringing in 2001. She was the first juvenile Osprey to fledge from a nest in central England for more than 150 years.

2002 – No More Translocations

With no further translocations planned in 2002, we were able to focus our activities on the careful monitoring and survey of returning Ospreys. Weekly 'coordinated watches' allowed us to build up a picture of the movements and activities of resident Ospreys and possible newcomers, and over the course of the season we were able to identify five Rutland-ringed males and one female either holding territory or present in the area.

The watches were held over four-hour periods either at dawn or before dusk. With six points around the reservoir being manned we were also able to build up a picture of foraging behaviour. During the months of April and May, for example, with the warmer temperatures in the shallow lagoons on the reserve, individual Ospreys were frequently seen hunting, particularly over Lagoon 3 where there were large shoals of Roach. Later in the season the open water of the reservoir was the preferred hunting ground. A study by Tim Mackrill revealed considerable variations in hunt duration and number of dives, with wind speed and gustiness being the principal influencing factors behind the differences. Hunt duration, for example, ranged from as little as 10 minutes to well over an hour and although the vast majority of hunts culminated in a successful dive, birds on average needed one to five dives to successfully catch their prey.

Meanwhile at Site B a promising beginning to the season ended with a disappointing and unsuccessful outcome. For the second year running 03(97) was the first of the Rutland cohort to return and was present at the nest from 23 March. Some ten days later, following a period of dedicated nest building and repair, his mate, the unringed female, joined him and the ritual courtship behaviour began.

With incubation under way, we began 24-hour monitoring, allowing us to make a detailed study of the pair's behaviour and the roles undertaken by the male and female. As night fell the male would disappear into the wood behind the nest to roost, leaving the female to sit tight. With the aid of night-vision optical equipment, the other-worldliness of the countryside at night came alive, the stillness of the scene being punctuated by grazing Fallow Deer, Badgers, the occasional Fox and Tawny Owls. From time to time the female would fly over the wood in the middle of the night, circling over the crop fields to stretch her wings before returning to the nest. One night she appeared to have trouble landing on the nest in the pitch blackness, making three attempts before succeeding. Between 4 and 5am the male would return to the nest to give the female a brief respite, allowing her to stretch and preen.

A study of the data by a visiting Dutch student, Jody Ettema, concluded that by the end of the 41-day marathon, the female had undertaken 87.3% of the incubation and to our delight, on 5 June, she was rewarded with the first hatching. But our excitement was short-lived – five days of excessively wet weather followed and within days it was clear that any attempts to feed young had ceased. By 9 June the female was leaving the nest for longer than usual and the male didn't replace her, leaving the nest unoccupied for extended periods. This pattern continued and despite apparent half-hearted bouts of incubation of failed eggs, by 17 June the pair was absent from the nest for hours at a time. We were later able to confirm that three eggs had been laid and one chick had hatched before succumbing to the atrocious conditions.

Meanwhile in Manton Bay, 08(97) lived up to form with a series of dalliances during the course of the season. His unringed partner of the previous summer failed to reappear, and despite the brief appearance of another unringed sub-adult he remained unpaired for the critical breeding season. During this time he focused his energies on rather comical attempts to establish nest platforms on various electricity pylons in the vicinity, eventually succeeding in creating a small but unsteady platform on one. This appeared to be sufficient inducement to entice the young female back and she readily accepted fish from him throughout her summer at Rutland Water, suggesting a pair bond had developed.

A second female made two brief appearances in Manton Bay, both of which coincided with the previous incumbent's absences. Significantly this bird, 05(00), was the first translocated female to return to Rutland, having been released in 2000.

4/9/02 - 6.30pm
08 - probably last drawing of him before he leaves.

Volunteer Diary, Andy and Anne Strang, 2009

This was an exciting day. We were going to be the first volunteers to do a shift at Site N, a remote location deep in the Rutland countryside. It was also the first season that a pair of Ospreys had chosen to breed at this particular site. This was our fifth season as volunteers, having started in 2005, the year of the last translocation of chicks from Scotland. Being rookies everything about that 2005 season was totally new to us. We were initiated by John Wright and throughout that season did shifts at Manton Bay, Site B and in 'the outpost' at the bottom of Lax Hill, where we witnessed the fledging of the translocated chicks and followed their movement around the area using the yagi. All of that was very interesting and exciting at the time. But now, five years on, we were going to Site N where everything was new and 08(97) and 5N(04) were nesting for the first time. For us this was record-breaking stuff.

Although we had directions for getting to Site N we didn't know exactly where it was and what to expect when we eventually got there. So, when 21 April 2009 finally dawned, our feelings of excitement and expectancy were high. We'd been allocated the 9am to 1pm shift and, living over 30 miles away, and not being sure of the final part of the route, we didn't want to be late. So we were up at 6am and set off from home at 7am to allow for any unexpected traffic delays as well as a good half hour to park and walk into the site.

When we set out from Cosby it was a glorious bright sunny morning, but as we headed towards Uppingham it became increasingly misty until we were driving in fog with visibility down to about 20 metres. Turning off the A47 with visibility decreasing further we continued to follow our directions and despite the thickening mist finally managed to park the car and get ready to walk in to the site shortly after 8am. With visibility now down to a few metres we set off down a rough and deeply set narrow lane leading to Site N. We knew it would take about 30 minutes to reach the site, but there was nothing in the instructions to say that it might take much longer in 'adverse' weather conditions. However, it was a new adventure so we plodded on. Referring once more to the instructions, we were to look out for a turning to the right off the lane that would take us down a field and eventually to the hide. We carried on hopefully and although the mist was getting thicker the day appeared to be brightening up. As we continued down the track we were suddenly aware of a backlit figure, like a Brocken Spectre, standing on the right-hand side of the lane. As we approached, the spectre turned out to be Paul Stammers, who had come up from the hide to meet us and fix an arrow to a post, pointing out the direction to take to reach the hide. Everything was still shrouded in thick mist and although, when we reached the hide, Paul pointed out where the nest was we couldn't see it at all. By this time it was after 9am and officially we were on duty. But the only thing we could record was that the mist was so thick that we couldn't see the nest or even where it was located. As time went on we had occasional glimpses across the field through the mist, but we could see nothing that we could definitely identify as the nesting pole. Then, for just a moment, the mist cleared a little and for a few seconds we saw the nest pole and platform before they disappeared once more. Not wanting to miss anything, and with eyes glued to our binoculars, we focussed on the direction where we now knew the nest to be. Time went on and although the sun was now shining strongly there seemed to be no sign of the mist lifting. Then, just after 10am, suddenly and without warning, the curtain of mist rose and there before us lay a beautiful sun-drenched valley. 5N was clearly visible on the nest, which was located about 200 metres ahead on the fence line across a glowing golden field of oil-seed rape that stretched down to a fence line to the left of the hide, along which were numerous trees and shrubs, and upwards to the horizon on the right.

There was no sign of 08 and we surmised that he was either away fishing or hidden up on one or other of the many trees visible along the field boundaries. During the next hour we were kept busy recording multiple intrusions of unidentified male Ospreys with 5N in the absence of 08 vigorously flapping her wings to defend the nest. On several occasions the intruders, which were very aggressive, almost landed on the nest, but 5N managed to keep them at bay. Just before 11.30am 08 returned with a large trout and retired to a nearby perch, where he ate about half of the fish before taking the remainder to the nest. 5N then flew off to eat it on the horizontal T-perch while 08 took over incubation. Just after 12.20pm 5N returned to the nest with the remainder of the trout and resumed incubation, while 08 flew off towards the reservoir just before we ended our shift at 1pm.

Anne and I did other shifts at Site N in 2009 and 2010, but none as vivid and memorable as when the curtain of mist rose to reveal the sight of this magical valley on that first morning on 21 April 2009.

An Expanding Colony

When the project was first conceived in the mid-1990s Roy Dennis felt the Rutland Water area could support 8–10 pairs of breeding Ospreys. Our long-term aim, therefore, was to establish a self-sustaining breeding population that, in time, would aid the re-colonisation of other parts of southern Britain. So, although the successful fledging of the first chick in 2001 was clearly a major milestone for the project, long-term success could only be judged on the establishment of a Rutland Water colony. And that, we knew, would take time.

2003

The failure at Site B in 2002 demonstrated that we needed to be patient. Trying to re-establish a population of Ospreys was never going to be an overnight success. Research by Roy Dennis in Scotland has shown that young birds often have to wait five or more years before they breed for the first time. Then, once a pair becomes established, there is no guarantee that it will raise chicks every year.

03(97) remained faithful to Site B in 2003, returning to the nest in late March. Male Ospreys appear almost regal when they first return to their nests in late March, their gleaming white underparts glistening in the early-spring sunshine. Their arrival is a sure sign that summer is just around the corner.

Two weeks passed and 03(97) was still alone at the nest. Sadly it was becoming clear that his mate of the previous two years wasn't going to return. This added weight to a theory that she may have been an older breeding bird that had been ousted from the Scottish population. Perhaps her two years at Rutland Water had been a final fling and her advancing years had contributed to the failure in 2002? Whatever the case, her arrival had kick-started the Rutland population and probably emphasises that these older birds can be important in new and expanding Osprey colonies.

Female 05(00) at Site B. She was the first translocated female to breed and raised a total of 17 chicks with 03(97) over the course of six years.

So what would happen now? We wondered whether 03(97) would find a new mate. On 15 April a three-year-old female, 05(00), joined him at Site B. 05(00) had first returned to Rutland the previous July, spending two brief periods with 08(97) in Manton Bay. At the time we'd hoped that she would return to breed with 08(97), but with 03(97)'s mate not returning to Site B, 05(00) settled there instead. For the second time, 03(97) had outdone his compatriot from 1997.

05(00)'s return was significant for a number of reasons. Firstly, she was a translocated bird. Over the course of the six years that we released young Scottish Ospreys at the reserve, we only moved 15 females. As described earlier, this was based on evidence from the USA that males were more likely to return to their natal sites than females. For this reason 05(00)'s return was very encouraging. It was pleasing from a personal point of view too. Summer 2000 had been my second year as a member of the project team and I was thrilled to be invited up to Scotland with Helen McIntyre and Andy Brown of Anglian Water to help Roy Dennis collect the birds that year. Roy is an inspirational man and as an 18-year-old aspiring conservationist I felt privileged to have the opportunity to help him with this very important work. Having collected ten birds, Andy, Helen and I set off in the hired van with the birds in wine boxes in the back. One of those birds was 05(00), which made seeing her at Site B in spring 2003 all the more rewarding.

Three weeks after arriving at Site B, 05(00) laid a clutch of three eggs and we again began 24-hour monitoring of the nest. Meanwhile, something quite remarkable was happening nearby. On 28 April, 03(97)'s neighbour, 03(98), had been joined at Site C by a female, 06(01). Like 05(00) she was a translocated bird but, having been released in 2001, she was a year younger.

Male 03(97) delivering a large Bream to the Site B nest. Bream are bottom-feeding fish and the Ospreys usually only catch them in midsummer when they spend time basking on the surface.

The adult female does the majority of the incubating, with the male taking over for brief periods during the day to give her a break. Once the chicks hatch it is only the female who broods them.

Site B.
♀ brooding, ♂ just below nest
4.6.05.

We were surprised to see this young female so early in the season. Two-year-old Ospreys usually return later in the year, often arriving in late May or June before spending the rest of the summer exploring Rutland and further afield. However, 06(01) always seemed to buck the trend. One of 14 translocated juveniles equipped with satellite transmitters, she wintered on the Rio Tajo in Portugal. This in itself was not especially surprising – an increasing number of Ospreys from the UK winter in Iberia rather than flying further south into Africa – but what was unusual was that she returned to England less than a year later. In July 2002 she flew north through Yorkshire and then onto Northumberland. The last signal we received from her transmitter showed that she was close to St Abb's Head on 21 June. Unfortunately we received no further data and when she returned to Rutland the next spring we saw that the transmitter had fallen off.

There are no known records of two-year-old Ospreys breeding in the UK, but that didn't stop 06(01). On 22 May she laid a clutch of at least two eggs in the Site C nest, breaking another record in the process. She had now laid the latest clutch of eggs recorded on these shores.

By late June there were three healthy chicks at the Site B nest and incubation was nearing an end at Site C. Eventually we observed the magical moment when the female first offers fish down into the nest. For the first time we now had two nests with chicks.

Both nests continued to be monitored by volunteers. I was one of them, having completed my degree at the University of East Anglia. It was wonderful to be able to visit both nests on the same day and chart the development of the young birds. Roy Dennis came down to help us ring the Site C chicks in August and we were pleased to see the youngsters in good condition. A few weeks later they fledged successfully. They were so late that their tentative first flights coincided with the fields surrounding the nest being harvested. In the early years we used to worry about this kind of disturbance but we've since found that the birds are usually tolerant of agricultural work. Tractors and combine harvesters can work within 50 metres of nests and the birds will ignore them. They only seem to feel threatened if a vehicle stops and the driver gets out of the cab. Fortunately all the landowners we work with are extremely conscientious and there are rarely any problems. There certainly weren't any at Site C and the two youngsters quickly grew in confidence on the wing.

The Site C chicks lingered well into September, but by the end of the month both birds had set out on migration. With all three juveniles successfully fledging from Site B too, it had been a very encouraging few months. After the disappointments of the previous year, 2003 had proved to be a great summer.

28·3·04

03 had baler twine caught on his leg
this afternoon. He took off, the twine got
snagged on branches + he hung upside
down below nest for several seconds
before he broke free. Twine now hanging from nest.

2004

As every spring, expectations were high in 2004. Following
the successes of the previous year we were hopeful that the
breeding population would continue to grow.

Having graduated from university the previous summer
I was now working as a Field Officer on the project. On
15 April, with 03(97) back at Site B, I decided to spend a
few hours there. 05(00) had arrived in Rutland that day
the previous year and I wondered if she would do it again.
I arrived at Site B to find 03(97) snoozing next to the nest,
holding a partly eaten fish.

Not much happened for the next hour. A Red Kite
lolloped lazily over the nest and a Nuthatch called loudly
above my head, but 03(97) barely moved. Suddenly, though,
he took off from the nest and rose almost vertically, legs

dangling. His shrill display call suggested that he'd seen
a female and I frantically scanned the horizon with my
binoculars. There, arriving from the south-east, was another
Osprey – a female. My heart was pounding. She headed
straight for the nest and as she landed I glimpsed a green
ring. 03(97) continued to display high above the nest and
eventually the female moved to a position where I could read
the ring. As I had hoped, it was 05(00). She had arrived on
exactly the same day as the previous year. I immediately
phoned John to tell him and over the phone he said he could
hear 03(97) displaying. It was a wonderful moment and one
I will always remember. Eventually 03(97) landed on the nest
and presented the fish to the female.

Having raised three chicks the previous year, 03(97) and
05(00) settled back into breeding mode immediately. Sadly,
though, things were different at Site C. 03(98) was back on
territory but by early May there was still no sign of 06(01).

Perhaps breeding at such a young age had taken its toll on her. We never saw her again and could only presume that she had died during the winter. That disappointment was compounded by the fact that none of the other translocated males attracted mates. Both 08(97) and 09(98) now had established territories, but neither bred. 08(97) was joined by an unringed female for almost two weeks in early April, but she departed just as we were beginning to think that she would stay.

This was becoming a familiar story. Passing Scottish females would arrive in early April and stay for a few days. During their brief sojourns in Rutland they would readily accept fish from males eager to impress and some even helped with nest building. Then, after a day or so, they would be off, never to be seen again. It went against our original project rationale and was a worrying trend.

Juvenile male 5R(04) fledged in mid-July and was the first Rutland-bred juvenile to return to the area two years later.

5R(04) and 5N(04) in the Site B nest, aged around ten days. Both birds subsequently returned to Rutland Water.

Site B - 24·7·04

03(97) missing since 06·10hr. From 08·45 there have been 3-4 intruding ♂ ospreys around the nest. At 09·45 i saw an orange ringed ♂, Red 02 + a very tatty ♂? all above the nest + landing in nearby trees. Then from between 10·30 - 12 the nest ♀ corvorted with red 02, sometimes chasing him but other times just casually circling with him. Then at 12·20pm 03 returned (no fish) + began chasing them all. 08(97) then returned and began dive bombing 03 + ♀ on nest. 03 went up and chased 08 off, both ♂'s going high South. Red 02, 09(98) + 03(98) now back over nest at 12·50. Nearby combine harvesting is not helping as it keeps flushing the ♀ and ♂'s get excited.
13·20 - Red 02 now landed in top of conifer behind nest - he is a real trouble maker.
14·00 - All is quiet once again apart from the combine harvester.

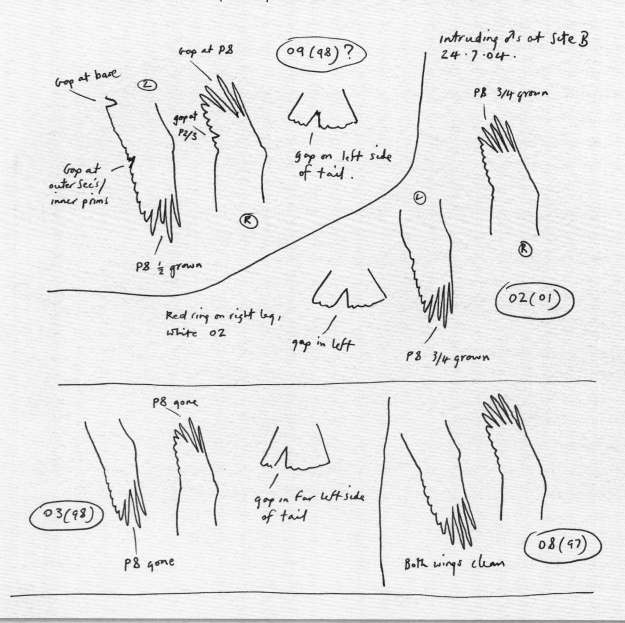

intruding ♂'s at site B
24·7·04.

These females knew that staying at a nest for a few days resulted in free meals, and that was all they were interested in.

Fortunately things were different at Site B. 03(97) and 05(00) raised two healthy chicks – a male and a female – and when we ringed them on a damp morning in early June we found them to be in superb condition. They were fitted with green colour rings on their right legs. By late July they were both on the wing and growing in confidence by the day. As it turned out these two young Ospreys – 5R(04) and 5N(04) – would later play a pivotal role in the future growth of the colony.

As the summer progressed the non-breeding males, now less tied to their own territories, began to make frequent intrusions at Site B. 08(97), 03(98) and 09(98) all became regular visitors, sometimes sitting on trees close to the nest.

It was clear that Site B was now the prime site in the colony and the one that all the birds wanted to have as their own.

The presence of these non-breeding males demonstrated that things were not going according to plan. The fact that passing Scottish females appeared reluctant to stay and breed was concerning. With this in mind we put together a proposal to translocate more female chicks from Scotland in 2005. By the latter part of 2004, we had six non-breeding males in Rutland and we felt that the population needed an extra boost of females. 05(00) and 06(01) had demonstrated that translocated females would come back and breed and we hoped that by releasing more females we could redress the current bias towards males. SNH agreed and granted a special one-off licence for a release in 2005. Roy kindly agreed to collect the birds for us once again.

Male 06(00) displaying. When displaying Ospreys repeatedly rise, then stoop at high speed whilst giving a high-pitched call.

2005

Events in spring 2005 appeared to justify our decision to release more females. 03(97) and 05(00) returned to Site B, but again they were the only breeding pair. Several females arrived in early April, but again, none stayed to breed. Perhaps they were all established breeders from Scotland? Once successful at a nest most Ospreys remain faithful to that site and, as in previous years, these females were probably only lingering for the free fish. The one exception was a female who appeared on 28 April. Her late arrival suggested she didn't have a nest further north or had been ousted from one by another bird and, sure enough, she summered in Rutland, moving between the territories of 08(97) and 09(98).

Female 05(00) incubating at Site B, while her mate was away fishing. During the breeding season male and female Ospreys have very clearly defined roles.

♀ 05 – Site B
28.5.05

Quite restless today – hatching due tomorrow (38 days)

During hot, sunny weather female Ospreys protect their offspring by shading them from the sun.

constantly panting

♀ Shading young from sun

3 wks old today

19.6.05
Site B
28f° today

03(97) and 05(00) at Site B, 4 April 2005. The male returned ten days before his mate and spent the time rebuilding the nest after it had suffered weather damage over the winter.

08(97) on the Site C nest, May 2005. 08 was the first translocated bird to return to Rutland, and spent several years attempting to attract females to various nest sites in the area.

Juvenile 30(05) preparing for her first flight. She returned to Rutland two years later and raised chicks of her own for the first time in 2009.

Preparing the release site for the arrival of the translocated Ospreys, 5 July 2005.

Translocated juveniles before making their first flights, 3 August 2005.

Translocated juvenile taking to the air for the first time, 3 August 2005.

Juvenile females being released in 2005. The initial translocations between 1996 and 2001 involved 49 males but only 15 females. Advice from the United States had suggested that males were more likely to return to the release area. However, our subsequent experience suggested a 50:50 split would have resulted in a faster rate of population growth, so we were granted a special one-off licence in 2005 to release an extra batch of females. Sadly, none of them subsequently returned.

08 (97) around Lax hill.

3.8.05.

He came 2-3 times to attack the translocated juvs.

♂ 08(97) dive bombing of the released juvenlies would often result in him actually striking the juvs. On one occasion he knocked 4 juveniles of AN1

08 with our fish.

Juvenile 7A preparing for dive bomb.

dead tree on edge of wood

For around a week after the translocated juveniles were released in 2005, 08(97) – who was holding territory in nearby Manton Bay – showed considerable aggression, repeatedly dive-bombing them around the Lax Hill release site.

By July the young female was spending most of her time with 08(97) in Manton Bay and this coincided with the arrival of 11 translocated Ospreys from Scotland – nine females and two males. We had now refined our translocation techniques and all 11 birds were successfully released at the end of the month. Sadly one of the birds disappeared immediately after release but, as in previous years, the other ten birds remained close to Lax Hill. The one major difference from the earlier releases was that there were now far more adult Ospreys in the area. We wondered how the adult birds would react to the presence of the newly released translocated birds.

08(97) made his presence felt straightaway. He left the Manton Bay nest to dive-bomb the juveniles as soon as they'd made their first flight. This aggression was surprising. The young birds posed no threat to 08(97), but he clearly didn't see it that way. His ferocious dive-bombing made for spectacular, if worrying, viewing from 'the outpost' as we watched the young birds leave the safety of the release pens for the first time. First flights are difficult enough, but having an adult Osprey chasing you around Lax Hill was not an ideal introduction to life in the air.

Fortunately the reaction of the young female who had arrived in late April was completely different. As in previous years the juveniles favoured AN1 – an artificial nest on Lax Hill – during the first few days after release. The nest was easily accessible from the air and provided a relatively simple landing spot. Every time an adult bird flew over this nest, the assembled juveniles food-begged incessantly. 08(97) ignored these food-begging calls, but the female reacted very differently. Two days after the first youngsters had been released, the female delivered a fish to the juveniles on the nest. Their calls had obviously triggered a maternal instinct in her and, even though she was not related to any of the translocated birds, it seemed that she felt compelled to feed them. She continued to deliver fish to juveniles on AN1 and another artificial nest on the south side of Lax Hill for the next three weeks, providing more than 25 fish in the process. Her behaviour contrasted greatly with that of 08(97), who continued to dive-bomb the juveniles for several weeks.

It was not just 08(97) and the young female who were attracted to Lax Hill by the presence of the translocated birds. 09(98) was back for his sixth summer in Rutland and he made regular visits to Lax Hill following the release of the juveniles. Unlike 08(97) and the female, though, he did not appear overly interested in the birds themselves; he was there for the fish. He collected fish that we'd put out for the juveniles on many occasions, often remaining to eat it alongside the youngsters. One of the most rewarding aspects of the project is that we get to know the birds as individuals and the differing behaviour of the three adult birds was fascinating to observe.

7N

7B

7C

unringed f

Lax Hill –
30·7·05.

unringed f (U4) perched just
behind released Juveniles on AN1.
She is regularly dropping fish, usually
half-eaten ones into nest + the juvs
are eating them.

In contrast to 08(97), an unringed adult female who spent several months
at Rutland Water in 2005 delivered fish to the newly released juveniles.

♂ 09(98) Stealing food from the translocated Juveniles. He showed
no aggression towards the Juveniles unlike 08(97)

Lax hill – 14·8·05.

09(98) showed no
aggression to the
translocated juveniles,
but visited the release
pens for fish.

03(97) having just returned to Site B in spring 2006. He is usually among the first birds to return to Rutland each year.

03 97
25.3.06.

looking very smart as usual.
07.32.

2006

Having released the 11 birds in 2005 we knew we would have to wait until at least 2007 before any of them returned. But 2006 was notable for the return of two of our own 'home-grown' Ospreys. We hoped that the translocation in 2005 would give the colony a small but significant demographic boost, but we knew that the long-term viability of the population would depend on our own Rutland-fledged chicks returning to breed themselves. What happened in 2006, therefore, was most encouraging. From a personal point of view the year was also memorable because

I was now employed as full-time Project Officer.

As we were now coming to expect, 03(97) and 05(00) returned to Site B in the spring, and as in the previous two years, they were the only breeding pair. Prior to the arrival of 05(00), a passing Scottish female had lingered for a couple of days with 03(97), but she soon moved on. As soon as 05(00) returned, normal service was resumed. She and her now very experienced mate raised another three chicks, demonstrating what an important breeding pair they were becoming. This was further emphasised by events later in the summer.

03 nest scraping One of the first jobs.
Backward scraping like a scratching chicken.
The nest is in quite a state, the east side is completely open.
25.3.06.

lovely sunny early am.

bits of wood flying out.

One of the first jobs for male Ospreys when they return to their nest in the spring is to scrape out the nest cup. In 2006 the nest had suffered severe wind damage during the winter.

08'97.
Manton Bay
27·3·06.

14·02

Arrived on 24-3, first seen
Fishing North Arm at
4pm.

virtually no eyebrows
as usual. Left
one slightly
better marked

In March 2006, 08(97) once again
returned to his territory in Manton
Bay. As the summer progressed he
would often wander away from
the bay and take up temporary
residence on other artificial
nests elsewhere.

well marked
breast band.

In Rutland, Ospreys usually line their nests with turf
but sometimes take advantage of rotting bales of
straw, snatching clumps to take back to the nest.

♂ 03 just about to take a chunk of straw.
from some large rotting bales.

1·4·06

10 am

It's easy to see how baling twine ends up in nests.

11.6.06 —
Unidentified ♂ Fishing in North Arm at 17.00hr. Green ring on right leg could point to it
being 2004 Site B chick 5R!. He flew west into Fishponds but carried on. Time will tell.

On 11 June, John Wright and Information Officer Paul Stammers were leading a guided Osprey fishing watch on the Hambleton Peninsula. With the Site B nest situated on private land, this was one of the most reliable places to see Ospreys at the reservoir. At around 5pm, not long after they'd set up telescopes on the shoreline, a male Osprey began fishing in front of them. As you would expect, everyone in the group was excited to see an Osprey in action, but there was no one more excited than John when he realised the significance of the bird. Over the years John has developed an unparalleled knowledge of every individual Rutland Osprey and is able to identify each bird by plumage and moult. He quickly noted that this bird had a green ring, but more significantly, its moult was different from that of the only green-ringed Osprey that had been present in Rutland that summer, 06(00). Two years previously we'd ringed the Site B chicks with green rings on their right legs. Could this male be 5R(04), who fledged from Site B that year? John ran off down the shoreline in hot pursuit of the bird, but he couldn't get any closer and the bird headed off towards the dam and out of sight. For the time being its identity would have to remain a mystery.

Fortunately it was a mystery that didn't take long to solve. Two days later I received an email from Keith Burtonwood, a keen photographer from the Midlands. He had photographed an Osprey at Coombe Abbey near Coventry shortly after first light on the day John had seen the mystery male in the North Arm. I opened up the photo and to my amazement could see a green ring on the bird's right leg. By zooming in on the photo we could just about make out the inscription on the ring. It was 5R(04). Keith had photographed 5R(04) around ten hours before John saw the green-ringed bird at Rutland Water – easily enough time for it to fly the 35 or so miles to Rutland – so it had to be the same one. Fantastic!

Over the course of the next few months we identified 5R(04) at various locations around Rutland. Two-year-old Ospreys are too young to establish a territory, so they usually spend the summer exploring. Recent satellite-tracking and ringing studies have shown that our birds probably wander all over England – explaining the sporadic nature of our sightings of 5R(04) that summer and also the fact that he'd been photographed at Coombe Abbey.

03(97) on the Site B nest, 8 April 2006.

Adult female on the Site B nest with her three two-and-a-half-week-old chicks. The male is alarm calling below – a sure sign that an intruding Osprey is approaching.

The Site B juveniles a few weeks after fledging, 10 August 2006.

5R(04) shortly after his return to Rutland, 7 August 2006. He was the first Rutland-bred Osprey to return.

We were thrilled that 5R(04) had made it back to Rutland Water. It was another very significant step forward and encouraging for the long-term viability of the population.

As in previous years 08(97) had spent most of his summer at the artificial nest in Manton Bay. It had been a lonely few months for him. We'd hoped that the young unringed female who had paired with him in 2005 would return, especially given that she had acted so maternally towards the translocated juveniles during August. Sadly, though, it didn't happen – perhaps she didn't survive the winter? Whatever the case, 08(97) was alone at Manton Bay once again.

On 15 July Information Officer Martin Blee was on duty at the Lyndon Visitor Centre. Late in the morning Martin received a report that a female Osprey had joined 08(97) in the bay. Martin raced down to Waderscrape Hide, hoping he might be able to identify the bird before it flew off. He rang John Wright and the bird was still there when they arrived at the hide. They immediately saw that it had a green ring on its right leg. Frustratingly the ring was partly obscured, and they couldn't read the inscription. A nervous few minutes passed before the bird hopped back on to the edge of the nest. It was 5N(04). Amazingly, 5R(04)'s sister from 2004, 5N(04), had made it back too. John and Martin were elated. Up until now 08(97) had always had liaisons with Scottish females, but here was a young Rutland bird who knew nothing of Scotland. She wouldn't be flying any further north. Or at least we hoped that she wouldn't.

As it turned out, 5N(04) spent the rest of the summer with 08(97), rarely venturing far from the Manton Bay nest. By late August she was helping her new mate to add nest lining to the huge structure and we felt confident that she would return next spring. Elsewhere several unringed females

18.7.06 – scorching hot day.

Had a nice session with 08 + 5N in Manton Bay from 05.30 hr – 0800. She caught a Large Trout right next to the nest at 06.20. Then Suddenly, 08 appeared, holding the remains of a Fish. Both sat side by side eating on the T-perch. She then left half of the trout flopped over the perch and 08 flew to the nest and began rearranging sticks. 5N then joined him on the nest but no sooner had she landed, 08 left and stole the trout that she had left balancing on the perch. He then sat eating it like it was his own. Good old 08, nothing changes !!
1 fresh White-letter Hairstreak in Lax hill, Sunbathing on Sycamore's.

While at the Site B nest in the afternoon, the adult female alarm called and 5N flew over. Both Females (mother + daughter!) circled together over the nest area before both drifted north. ♂03 had only just returned with a Roach and seemed more bothered with eating than chasing.

TOP 5N(04) (left) eating a trout at the Manton Bay nest, 18 July 2006.

MIDDLE Having eaten half of the fish, 5N(04) left it balanced over the perch.

BOTTOM 5N(04) then flew to the nest to join 08(97), but he flew straight to the perch to steal the fish.

black mask

very dark forehead

very dark breast band

Over the course of summer 2006, two unringed females spent time in Rutland. It is likely they were two-year-old Scottish birds, returning to the UK for the first time.

new unringed ♀
11·6·06.
suddenly landed on the Site C nest.
09 eventually brought partial bream to her.

Unringed ♀ - 23·7·06
calling her U9
She is moving between ♂09 + ♂06.

Flecks

Greater Coverts growing fast. Most of these have appeared within a week.

visited Rutland and flirted with the unattached males, notably 09(98) and 06(00).

Once the birds have migrated south in the autumn Rutland has a strangely empty feel about it. The birds that have been a part of our lives every day since late March have suddenly departed. Once they had gone in September 2006, though, it provided us with an opportunity to carry out some very important work at Site B. When we ringed the chicks in June we noticed that the branches supporting the huge nest appeared rotten. There have been numerous examples in Scotland of Osprey nests collapsing during the breeding season and that was the last thing we wanted to happen at Site B, especially as the nest had become the cornerstone of the Osprey colony in Rutland. So, with this in mind, we called for help. Mark Ashman, a local tree surgeon, kindly

offered to come and have a look at the tree for us using the mobile elevated platform – or cherry picker – that he uses for his tree surgery work. Mark confirmed our fears that the nest was in danger of collapsing. There was only one thing for it – we needed to take the top out of the tree and rebuild the nest. Over the past 50 years Roy Dennis has rebuilt many Scottish nests and we knew that lowering the structure slightly would have no impact on the success of the site. So Mark and Garry Jones, another tree surgeon friend of the project, set about the job. Using his chainsaw Garry removed the top 2 metres of the tree, causing the nest to come crashing down. He then fixed a large circular piece of external plywood to the tree and rebuilt the nest, using 03(97)'s own sticks. Within a couple of hours we had a new nest that we knew wouldn't collapse next summer. A job well done.

09(98) at Site B following the departure of 03(97) and his family, 12 September 2006. After he had gone we rebuilt the nest in a stronger part of the tree as a visit earlier in the season had revealed that the branches supporting the nest were rotten.

The nest tree with the rotten uppermost branches removed.

The old nest prior to us rebuilding it.

Local tree surgeon Garry Jones putting the finishing touches to the new nest.

03(97) having just returned to the rebuilt Site B nest, 26 March 2007.

2007

In many ways one of the most captivating aspects of the project is that the birds only spend half their year in Rutland. Even though ringing and satellite tracking of the birds have revealed a great deal about their migration to West Africa, there is still an element of mystery about their lives. By spring an air of expectancy descends on Rutland as we await the return of the first birds. There wouldn't be that same sense of anticipation in late March if they were present all year.

Spring 2007 was especially exciting because we knew that, at long last, 08(97) had every chance of breeding for the first time. In view of this we carried out major refurbishments to the Lyndon Visitor Centre over the winter. We knew that if the birds did breed in Manton Bay, it would generate a huge amount of interest. 08(97) returned to the nest in late March and on Good Friday, 6 April, we opened the doors to visitors for the first time. I remember standing in the centre that morning chatting to people from all over England about our hopes for the year. Suddenly our conversation was interrupted by a radio message from volunteer Mark Sims who was in Shallow Water Hide. A female Osprey had just landed on the nest! As luck would have it, Tim Appleton had just arrived at the centre and we rushed down to the hide in his Land Rover. Mark was sure that the female had a green ring on her right leg and almost as he said it she lowered her leg and we could read the inscription. It was 5N(04). I think the only individual more pleased to see her than Tim

and I was 08(97). He spent the next 45 minutes displaying spectacularly above the bay, rising and falling like a roller coaster, all the time uttering his distinctive high-pitched display call. Eventually 08(97) landed next to 5N(04) on the nest and we left them to it. With 03(97) and 05(00) back at Site B for what would be their fifth year breeding together, we now knew that for the first time in four years, we would have two breeding pairs again.

03(97) and 05(00) settled down to incubation in late April and as in the previous year we began the 24-hour vigil. But now, of course, we had a dilemma – should we try and guard two nests? The introduction of custodial sentences had reduced the number of active egg collectors, but could we risk leaving the Manton Bay nest unattended at night? Given that the nest is situated on a pole set in 2 metres of water it would be extremely difficult to climb, but egg collectors are determined people. Guarding two nests simultaneously wouldn't be easy, but after much discussion we decided to try it. Fortunately we had an extremely dedicated team of more than 100 volunteers to call on and, with additional help from Senior Warden Martyn Aspinall and his team, we managed to cover every night at both nests.

It's fair to say that night shifts at Manton Bay were not especially comfortable. We did it all from our trusty Land Rover. One person sat in the driver's seat scanning the shoreline with the night-vision telescope, while the other nightwatchman attempted to get some sleep on an old mattress slung in the back. Nightwatchman George Batchelor had one particularly uncomfortable night when heavy rain started leaking in through the roof. But all those

08(97) delivering the remains of a trout to the Manton Bay nest, 12 June 2007. Anglian Water stock the reservoir with both Rainbow and Brown Trout.

08(97) and 5N(04) landing on the Manton Bay nest, 7 April 2007.

08(97) (right) peering into the Manton Bay nest shortly after his first chick had hatched on 4 June. After several years of trying he was finally raising a family of his own.

Ringing the Manton Bay chicks, 13 July 2007.

5N(04) with her two chicks (female on left, male on right), 22 July 2007.

08 and 5N – Manton Bay – 18.6.07

uncomfortable nights were worth it when on 3 June 08(97) brought a fish back to the nest and 5N(04) offered food down into the nest cup for the first time, a sure sign that the first chick had hatched.

We had a camera on the shoreline that sent live images back to the Lyndon Visitor Centre, but we didn't have a camera looking directly into the nest, so that for the next two weeks the birds kept us guessing. How many chicks had hatched? Volunteers monitoring from Waderscrape Hide watched intently at feeding time for any clues. Eventually it was possible to make out the downy heads of two chicks.

By the time Osprey chicks are six weeks old they are just about fully grown, but still around two weeks away from making their first flight. This is the best time to ring them. Ringing the two chicks at Manton Bay in 2007 was no easy task. With the nest situated more than 6 metres above the water on a telegraph pole we needed a boat and triple extending ladder to reach it. Myself, Tim Appleton, John Wright and intrepid volunteer Ron Follows got to Lyndon early on 13 July and gently chugged out across Manton Bay. As usual both adult birds circled above our heads, but neither showed any signs of aggression. Once positioned under the pole we had to manhandle the ladder up and out of the boat, into the 2 metres of water below us and up onto the side of the nest. Ron then carefully climbed out of the boat, onto the ladder and up to the nest. It wasn't easy but we managed it.

At this age Osprey chicks are fairly easy to sex: females are generally bigger, more well marked and with chunkier bills and legs. Ron ringed the first chick – a female – and I ringed the second, a male. The male had an incredibly white head that made him look very like 08(97), whose most distinctive feature was a lack of well-defined 'eyebrows'.

Two weeks later the two Manton Bay youngsters made their first flights. With three chicks fledging at Site B – where 03(97) had returned to the rebuilt nest in the spring – we had matched our best ever year. Encouragingly, two other females had paired up with translocated males late in the summer. It was clear that, at last, the population was beginning to get established.

5N feeding chick (about 2 wks old) 18.6.07.

2008

It is inevitable that when you work with wildlife, there will be disappointments. Sadly, that was the case in 2008, although the year had started off extremely encouragingly. 08(97) and 5N(04) returned to Manton Bay and then, in what we thought could be a sign of things to come, two young males set up territory nearby. 5R(04) took over an artificial nest on the south side of Lax Hill, about a kilometre from his sister's nest. Meanwhile, 32(05) – who fledged from Site B in 2005 – took up residence on an artificial nest halfway between the two. In Scotland and elsewhere in the world Ospreys often nest very close together – sometimes just a few hundred metres apart – and it was incredible to be able to sit in the hides at Lyndon and see three occupied territories in such close proximity.

09(98) perched on the Site B nest prior to the arrival of 03(97). Ospreys prefer to take over established nests, rather than build their own.

08(97) and 5N(04) nest building in Manton Bay, April 2008. Males do the majority of nest building in the spring, but females also add sticks and, particularly, nest-lining material prior to laying the eggs.

09(98) perched in the North Arm of Rutland Water having been ousted by 03(97) from Site B, 14 April 2008.

08(97) and 5N(04) nest building in Manton Bay, April 2008.

5N(04) incubating at Manton Bay, 22 April 2008.

By late April, 5N(04) and 08(97) had begun incubating but neither 5R(04) nor 32(05) had attracted a mate. As time progressed 32(05), in particular, began to cause problems at the Manton Bay nest, trying to land on it several times a day. If 08(97) was present he would quickly see off the intruding male, but when he was away fishing 5N(04) was sometimes forced to leave the eggs unattended while she chased the young upstart away. This was exacerbated a few days into incubation when 08(97) disappeared for more than 48 hours. During this time he made two very brief visits to the nest, but otherwise left 5N(04) to fend for herself. Not only did this mean that she went without fish, but it also forced her to leave the eggs unattended for a total of more than five hours. Given that Ospreys rarely leave their eggs uncovered for more than a few minutes, this was an extremely worrying development. Eventually 08(97) returned to the nest and resumed normal duties, but we feared the damage had been done.

Sure enough, the eggs failed. As the expected hatching time approached we watched the behaviour of the female closely. Twice she appeared to be behaving as if a chick was hatching, but she never offered fish down into the nest – usually a sure sign that the first chick has hatched. Without a camera looking into the nest we couldn't be sure what was happening but it was possible that the chicks were too weak to survive the rigours of hatching. The underlying reason for 08(97)'s long absence at the start of incubating was also a mystery. We speculated that perhaps he'd found an unattached female elsewhere, but despite extensive searching, we never found one. Whatever the case, it seemed that it was his absence, combined with repeated intrusions by 32(05), which resulted in the failure of the nest.

Ospreys usually remain faithful to the same nest and mate each year. Mating begins within a few hours of their return in the spring.

♂ 06(00) bathing – 17·4·08 – 17·45hr.

06(00) bathing. Ospreys do not predate birds so wildfowl, such as these Shelducks, usually ignore them, knowing they are not a threat.

Non-breeding male 32(05) intruding at the Manton Bay nest, 3 May 2008. His repeated intrusions while 08(97) was absent resulted in the eggs failing to hatch.

The Site B family at fledging time, 21 July 2008.

Male 32(05) with a metal-ringed Scottish female from Argyll (left) on an artificial nest near Heron Hide. She returned to breed at Site O with 06(00) in 2009.

Fortunately there was better news at Site B, where 03(97) and 05(00) took their tally of chicks raised together to 17. Sadly one of their three chicks disappeared shortly after fledging, but the remaining two youngsters – a male and a female – both appeared in good condition when they departed. Of the two the female, 03(08), appeared the more independent and it was no surprise that she was the first to leave. John Wright was there to see her head south. Although this would prove to be the last time any of us would see her at Rutland Water, she was later to become a very important bird elsewhere. Her brother, 05(08), was more of a malingerer. He food-begged incessantly into early September and his father eventually appeared to lose patience. Every year previously 03(97) had waited until the last of his offspring had headed south before beginning his own journey, but on 30 August he clearly decided that enough was enough; 03(97) left his remaining chick to fend for himself. 05(00) remained at the nest for another three days, before eventually departing on 2 September.

Elsewhere two other non-breeding pairs remained on territory during the summer and a metal-ringed Scottish female made a brief visit, attracting the attention of both 5R(04) and 32(05).

Despite the disappointment of the Manton Bay nest failing there were still plenty of reasons for optimism at Rutland Water. In 2008 work started on a multimillion-pound project to create new wetland habitat at the reservoir. Nine new shallow-water lagoons were to be constructed to provide more habitat for the thousands of wildfowl that visit each year. Part of the work involved constructing a large dam across Manton Bay. This would, in effect, create a new Manton Bay lagoon that was separate from the main reservoir and enable us to manipulate water levels to within a few centimetres. As part of the work Natural England requested that we move the Osprey nest in Manton Bay away from the construction site, to ensure that the birds weren't disturbed by the work. We did this over the winter, moving the nest closer to Manton Bridge. This kind of work has been carried out for many years in Scotland and we were confident it wouldn't have any effect on the birds.

08 + 5N – Manton Bay – 18.8.08 – Been a long summer for the failed pair.

5N(04) on the Site B nest having returned to Rutland before 08(97), 31 March 2009. If females arrive before their mates, they often visit other nests for food. In this instance 5N(04) was fed by her father at her natal nest.

2009

On 29 March 2009 a group of project volunteers and I spent the afternoon in Shallow Water Hide on the Lyndon Nature Reserve. Sand Martins dashed back and forth in front of us, Chiffchaffs were in full song around the reserve and there was an air of expectancy – we knew an Osprey could appear at any time. Shortly after 5pm a group of Wigeon grazing the shoreline near the hide suddenly took to the air. An Osprey glided in from the south, circled the bay a couple of times and alighted on the new nest. It was 5N(04). For the first time she'd arrived back at Rutland before her mate. It was going to be interesting to see how she reacted to the new nest and also to being back before 08(97). Next day she spent very little time in Manton Bay and when 08(97) joined her a few days later, it was clear that neither bird was settled. Perhaps it was the nest's new location, or maybe just the fact that they had failed the previous summer. Whatever the case, their hesitancy was exacerbated by a pair of Canada Geese that seemed intent on trying to take over the nest. Geese are a perennial problem at the reservoir and if a pair becomes established at a nest early enough in the season then the Ospreys have great difficulty removing them. Sure enough 08(97) and 5N(04) began to spend time at an artificial nest away from the reservoir.

Two weeks later, 5N(04) laid a clutch of three eggs at the new site, which we called Site N. It was disappointing that they had moved away from the nest on the nature reserve, but this was tempered by the fact that the birds had chosen to breed on one of our artificial nests. That spring two other pairs began breeding on nests we had constructed.

Erecting a new artificial nest.

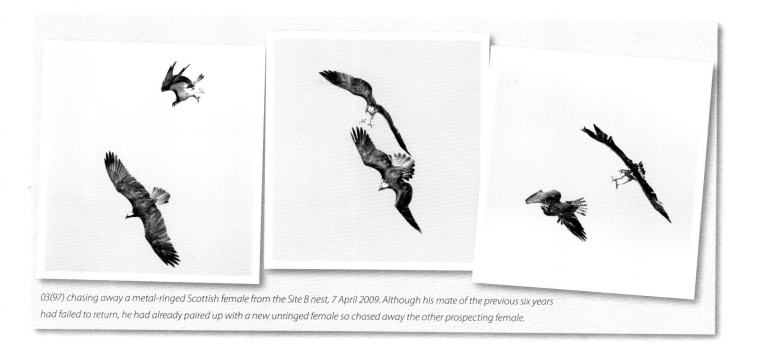

03(97) chasing away a metal-ringed Scottish female from the Site B nest, 7 April 2009. Although his mate of the previous six years had failed to return, he had already paired up with a new unringed female so chased away the other prospecting female.

Roy Dennis's work in Scotland has shown that the birds will readily use artificial nests, and it was rewarding to see it happening on nests we had built ourselves.

We decided to mount a 24-hour guard at Site N. 08(97) and his mate were now well-known birds and we felt it important to protect them. Sleeping quarters at Site N were a small tent located on a piece of flat ground behind the hide, and I joked at the annual volunteers' meeting that it would bring the 'best of British' out of those brave enough to forego a night's sleep to guard the nest. I was not disappointed – we quickly filled 40 night shifts and barring the odd person who had difficulty getting out of the tent at 2am in the morning, incubation passed without incident.

The first signs of hatching came at the end of May, and within a couple of weeks we could see two healthy chicks in the nest. We continued to monitor the nest closely, charting the development of the youngsters and recording fish deliveries to the nest. When we ringed the chicks six weeks after hatching we found them to be in fantastic condition. The youngsters were ringed with blue colour rings on their right legs – 03 and 04.

Unringed female visiting Manton Bay, 31 March 2009. After a four-day absence she returned to breed at Site B, having previously been seen intruding there as a sub-adult the previous summer.

5N(04) dive-bombing a Canada Goose at Manton Bay, 30 March 2009. Canada Geese often find Osprey nests safe places to rear young. If they get established before the Ospreys return, they can prove very difficult to evict.

08 carrying manure to Site N nest. 22.4.09.

Having failed to rear any young in Manton Bay in 2008, 08(97) and 5N(04) returned in spring 2009 to find Canada Geese attempting to take over their nest. This prompted them to move to a nearby artificial nest, known as Site N. After laying a clutch of three eggs, two chicks hatched and both fledged successfully. One of them, 03(09), returned to Rutland Water in 2011.

08 resting close to nest - 3.5.09

SN incubating 22.4.09

Fledging is an extremely challenging time for all young Ospreys but some are more confident than others. 03(09) not only fledged early – on 16 July – but was amazingly adept on the wing, venturing well away from the nest within a few days of taking to the air for the first time. His sister was more reluctant and fledged a week after her brother. She then disappeared for a very worrying 24 hours before volunteer Mick Lewin eventually located her perched almost half a mile from the nest.

We rarely see the young Ospreys catching fish before their first migration but 03(09) caught a trout on one of his many flights away from the nest. He was certainly a strong bird and we felt certain we would see him again.

Elsewhere 2009 was a real breakthrough year for the project. 03(97) again returned to Site B. Sadly 05(00) did not return, but our long-established star male paired up with a new unringed female – who had been seen intruding at Site B the previous summer – and raised two chicks. Two other pairs raised young, making 2009 easily the most successful year to date, with a total of nine chicks fledging from four nests.

The year was not without incident at Site B. By midsummer various non-breeding birds were making regular intrusions at the site, which posed a problem for 03(97). He needed to leave the nest unattended to go fishing, but whenever he did there was every chance that the non-breeding birds would cause problems for his mate. 03(97) often seemed reluctant to go fishing and this began to have a negative effect on his offspring. Two of the chicks developed well but it soon became apparent that the third

was considerably smaller – a runt. Sadly we found this third chick to be very weak when we visited the nest to ring the youngsters, and it died soon afterwards. 03(97) was having to invest so much time and energy into defending the nest that he simply wasn't catching enough fish to sustain all of his family.

From late July onwards, with her offspring now more independent, 03(97)'s mate was less tied to the nest. She took advantage of this by making numerous visits to Site C. Virtually every time she did so she was presented with a fish by 09(98). He was eager to impress the female, but her motivation was entirely selfish. As soon as she had a fish the female would return to Site B in order to feed her young. This continued for several days and as time went on the female began to spend longer at Site C. Eventually the two juveniles followed and 09(98) continued to catch fish for his adopted family. Although he never gave the fish directly to the juveniles, he accepted their presence on the nest and continued to provide fish for the female. 03(97), meanwhile, was powerless to do anything to stop it. He visited Site C, but each time was chased off by 09(98). He would return to Site B a forlorn figure. As time progressed the juveniles alternated between Site B and Site C, but the female rarely returned to Site B before she migrated in late August. Once she had gone 09(98) had no motivation to provide fish for the youngsters, so they began to spend longer periods with their father again. In a semi-colonial species like the Osprey, this kind of behaviour is probably not that unusual, but it certainly ensured that the juveniles were in good condition for migration.

07(09) landing on the Site O nest after her first flight, July 2009. Ospreys usually fledge when they are about 50–55 days old.

Site B female + both her juveniles food begging on the Site C nest !

site C
3-8-09

The Site B female has brought both the juveniles to 09 (98) nest. All three of them were food begging on his nest when I arrived. 09 arrived with a Trout but got flustered and landed briefly in a freshly ploughed field. He eventually took the fish to the nest but departed quickly, leaving them to squabble over it. I think he has bitten off more than he can chew. I nipped briefly to site B and ♂ 03 (97) was sitting quietly in the small oak - this is a very odd situation.

♂ 09 (98) with Trout

In late summer 2009, the Site B female and both her juveniles moved to Site C where they were fed by 09(98), the non-breeding male who had been on territory there all summer. The move appeared to be prompted by a lack of fish provided by the female's mate, 03(97).

03(97) sprawled over the edge of the Site B nest having been struck on the head by an intruding Scottish-ringed female. It was encouraging to see two non-Rutland females fighting over a nest in Rutland.

At long last it seemed that the population was moving forward. It appeared that with more birds in the area, Rutland was now proving a much more alluring prospect to passing Scottish birds than it had done a few years previously when there was a handful of inexperienced males on nests. Proof of this had come in the spring, when John Wright and I witnessed the most incredible aerial battle at Site B. By 7 April, the new unringed female had spent several days with 03(97) and it looked increasingly likely that she would stay to breed. John had seen her intruding at Site B the previous summer and with 05(00) still not back, she had a chance to take over an established nest site. Events that morning demonstrated that she wasn't the only female with this on her mind. Often the first indication that there is an intruding Osprey at a nest site is the shrill, high-pitched intruder call given by either male or female. The birds inevitably see an intruder before you do and on the morning of 7 April John and I heard that distinctive, plaintive 'chip' as we arrived at Site B. We scanned the sky and sure enough a female Osprey came into view. 03(97), who was perched next to his new mate, took off to chase away the intruding female. Often this is the sign for the intruder to make a hasty retreat. But not this bird; she was altogether more determined. Rather than heading off she became the aggressor, dive-bombing 03(97) and then the female on the nest. 03(97) retaliated and for the next 40 minutes or so John and I were treated to perhaps the most spectacular Osprey behaviour either of us have ever witnessed. All three birds became involved in the most incredible aerial tussle, diving at each other with talons outstretched and performing remarkable aerial acrobatics just above our heads. At one point the intruding female actually struck 03(97) and knocked him off the nest. So who was this female? During the scuffle we could see that she had a metal ring on her right leg and when John checked his photos of her underwing plumage he was able to confirm that it was a female who had recently arrived at Site O. Like the new Site B female, she had intruded at the nest the previous year and, while she had a potential mate at Site O, it seemed she was determined to make Site B her own. All the while, 09(98) was displaying high above Site B, hoping to lure the female to his own territory at Site C. The female wasn't interested in Site C, though – it was the prospect of breeding at a previously successful site that was behind her unrelenting persistence that morning. The fight seemed to go on and on.

The birds must have been exhausted and with the unringed female remaining resolutely on the nest, the intruding bird eventually gave up and returned to Site O. But this one incident had demonstrated, quite unequivocally, that Rutland was now an increasingly attractive breeding location for passing Scottish females. Later in the summer we set a hide up close to the Site O nest – where the female raised three chicks with 06(00) – and John was able to read the inscription on her metal ring, confirming that she was a three-year-old bird from Argyll in Scotland.

There was more room for optimism in June when a new unringed female arrived in Rutland. Her late arrival suggested that she was a two-year-old sub-adult bird and, sure enough, she spent most of the summer with 32(05) on the territory he'd established on an artificial nest situated in the middle of the newly constructed Lagoon 4 at Egleton.

32(05) (right) and unringed female, Lagoon 4, 18 July 2009. The pair spent the summer together at the nest and hopes were high they would return to breed there the next spring. However, following the disappearance of 32(05) in April 2010, the female bred with 5R(04) in Manton Bay.

2010

Spring 2010 arrived and, surprisingly, there was still no sign of the 2005 translocated birds. But encouragingly there was every indication that the population was becoming self-sustaining without them. Up until that year, every breeding pair had included at least one translocated bird, but that changed in 2010.

As we were coming to expect, 03(97) was the first bird back in Rutland, returning to Site B earlier than ever, on 19 March. He obviously knew that with several unattached males around, his territory was highly sought after.

One of the young birds clearly very intent on breeding was 32(05); he was back on territory on the newly constructed Lagoon 4 at Egleton on 22 March. Having arrived so early, the young male had free reign to visit the numerous other nests in the area. Over the next few days he only made sporadic visits to his own nest, preferring instead to spend time at Site N and Site O – both successful sites the previous summer. First 5N(04) and then the Site O female returned before their mates and 32(05) did his best to take advantage of this, delivering fish to both females following their arrival. 08(97) and then 06(00) were soon back, however, to evict him from their territories – 32(05) may have been eager to breed, but he was no match for an established breeding male.

Having been ousted from the two other territories we expected 32(05) to return to Lagoon 4, especially when the young female he had paired with the previous summer returned on 30 March. Strangely though, he did not. Several days passed and there was no sign of him. We began to wonder what had happened. With 32(05) absent from Lagoon 4 the young female moved to Manton Bay where she paired up with 32(05)'s elder brother, 5R(04). Despite the fact that

Unringed female (above) chasing 5N(04) at the Manton Bay nest, 9 April 2010. Having nested at Manton Bay in previous years, 5N(04) appeared reluctant to let another female settle there.

her new nest was several miles away, 5N(04) took objection to the new resident at her former nest. On 9 April we got a call from the volunteers monitoring the nest to say that a ferocious aerial battle was being played out in the bay. John Wright and I left the Lyndon Visitor Centre and rushed down to Shallow Water Hide. 5N(04) and the new Scottish female were embroiled in the most remarkable of tussles. 5N(04) was clearly the aggressor, but the new female was not about to relent. For the next seven hours the birds chased each other around the bay, sometimes at low level, but at other times so high that they were just specks in the sky above the Lyndon Nature Reserve. It made for compelling viewing. By dark 5R(04) was at the nest but there was no sign of either female. I went home worried. We were desperately hoping that at least one pair would breed on the reserve, and with 32(05) AWOL, Manton Bay appeared our best hope. But how would the young female react to the aggression of her neighbour? Would it force her to move elsewhere?

I woke up early next morning and got down to Manton Bay soon after first light. To my immense relief the female was back at the nest and there was no sign of 5N(04). Quite where she had been the previous evening we'll never know, but it was great to see her back. 5N(04) had also returned to her nest and it seemed that the two females had settled their dispute.

But none of this helped us to find out what had happened to 32(05). With his mate now settled with a rival male and his own territory vacant, we feared the worst. And things

5N(04) dive-bombing the new resident of the Manton Bay nest – an unringed female who had first appeared in Rutland the previous summer.

took even more of a downward turn on 6 April. On his daily checks of the nests John Wright had not seen 06(00) at Site O. This was worrying in itself, but what was concerning was that when he'd visited the nest in the evening, 06(00)'s mate was with AA(06). Like 32(05) and 5R(04), AA(06) was yet another Site B youngster and he too was back early and, it seemed, intent on breeding.

Next morning I was at the nest just after first light and once again AA(06) was with the female and there was no sign of 06(00). Like 32(05), he had just vanished. When 06(00) was still not back the next morning we knew something was wrong. Having raised three chicks at Site O the previous year there was no way he would choose to vacate the nest, or lose out to a younger male. So what had happened? Worryingly, we knew that both 32(05) and 06(00) fished the same, relatively small part of Rutland. Furthermore, neither was averse to visiting small lakes and ponds in the area, especially when the weather was inclement. One bird going missing you could explain, but for two established adult birds to simply vanish from the same part of Rutland within a few days of each other led us to fear that foul play could be involved. Despite extensive searching and police checks, our investigations came to nothing. We had lost two very important birds, but could do nothing about it.

5R(04) and unringed female (below) at Manton Bay, 6 April 2010. They became the first breeding pair not to include a translocated bird – a significant milestone for the project.

06(00), 8 April 2010, shortly before he disappeared in suspicious circumstances. That spring both 06(00) and 32(05) vanished within a few days of each other and were never seen again.

Fortunately, with an excess of males, we had birds to replace the ones we'd lost. At Site O, AA(06) paired with 06(00)'s mate, and the young female who had spent much of the previous summer with 32(05) settled in Manton Bay with 5R(04). This meant that at both nests we had breeding pairs that didn't include at least one translocated bird. In each case a wild-fledged Rutland male had paired up with a passing Scottish female. Not only did this show that the population was becoming self-sustaining, but it also backed up the original project rationale. Scottish females were now beginning to stop off and breed in the area.

The fact that we had an active nest on the nature reserve again was great news. Over the course of the summer more than 31,000 people visited the Lyndon Visitor Centre and many of them made the short walk down to Waderscrape Hide to enjoy spectacular views of the birds. One very exciting development was that we now had a camera looking directly into the nest, so that by late May the visitor centre was the place to be. Hatching at Osprey nests is usually quite predictable. The first egg to be laid usually hatches after around 36 days of incubation, so by late May we were scrutinising the female's every move for signs that a chick was about to appear. With hatching imminent, John Wright, Paul Stammers and I got to the visitor centre at 5am on 29 May. We cooked

5R(04) delivering a Roach to his family on the Manton Bay nest.

Manton Bay chicks at ringing, 13 July 2010.

breakfast and waited. By 8am there was no sign that a chick was about to hatch so we gave up, hoping that no one would realise how early we had got to the centre. The trouble is that the birds become such a huge part of your life when you're working on the project that it's impossible not to get this involved.

Another 24 hours passed and still there was nothing. We wondered if something had happened to the first egg. Next day Paul and I arrived at the visitor centre at around 7.30am. As usual the female was sitting tight on the nest when I switched the TV on. I rewound the footage we'd recorded overnight. The nightwatchmen had reported that just as it was getting light at 4.30am the female had become very restless. Surely a chick was hatching? We found the correct piece of footage. Bingo! A chick was emerging from one of the eggs. Although there are several other Osprey sites in the UK with cameras looking into nests, this was the first time that we'd seen one of our own chicks hatch on camera. It was one of those truly magical moments. I rang everyone I could think of, emailed the good news to the volunteers and put a post on the project's website. By mid-morning the visitor centre was full of people.

We all crowded round the television, captivated by the new arrival. For the first few hours the chick barely had the strength to hold its head upright for more than a few seconds, but now instinctively it was straining towards the female, hoping to be fed. 5R(04), who had watched the chick hatch from the side of the nest, had already delivered a good-sized trout to the female and the fish was now lying beside her in the nest. At 10.30am she stood up and inched her way carefully round to the fish. She tore up a piece and offered it to the chick, but she hadn't quite mastered the technique and was too far away from the chick for it to be able to take the tiny morsel of fish. This of course was the female's first experience of feeding and it showed. After another couple of failed attempts she moved a little closer to the new arrival and this time the youngster took the fish. Cheers of relief rang out around the visitor centre. Over the course of the next few hours both mother and chick became more confident and by the evening the youngster had enjoyed several good feeds. The timing of the hatching suggested that maybe the first egg was infertile, but as it turned out, both of the remaining two eggs hatched over the next couple of days. The Lyndon Visitor Centre buzzed with excitement as visitors, volunteers and staff alike watched the chicks growing in size and confidence by the day. And it wasn't just in the visitor centre that people could watch what was happening. We were also streaming the live images onto the project's website, allowing up to 4,000 people to follow the progress of the family each day from all over the world.

Elsewhere the other four breeding pairs also produced young. First-time breeder AA(06) raised three excellent chicks with his more experienced mate, 03(97) added three more youngsters to his Site B tally, 08(97) and 5N(04) produced another two chicks at Site N, and 08(01) and 30(05) raised a single chick at Site K. This meant that by early September 12 young Ospreys were heading south from Rutland Water. In other words, the Ospreys breeding in Rutland were now producing as many offspring as we translocated in any one year; another sure sign that, at last, the project was working well.

Site O juveniles preparing for their first flights, 18 July 2010.

2011

I find that one of the most rewarding aspects of the project is that we get to know the Ospreys as individuals. We try not to anthropomorphise too much, but it's inevitable that certain birds become real favourites over the years. One such bird was 08(97). Not only was he the first translocated Osprey to return, but also his repeated failed attempts to attract a mate were played out in front of thousands of people on the Lyndon Nature Reserve. Then of course when he finally did attract a mate, it was a Rutland-fledged female – and the first one to breed at that. You can imagine how sad we all were, therefore, when he disappeared in spring 2011. 08(97) returned to Site N on 29 March, a few days later than 5N(04). Within a few weeks 5N(04) had laid a clutch of eggs and, as usual, the birds were sharing incubation duties. By now we'd decided that it wasn't necessary to guard the Site N nest round the clock, but John Wright continued to monitor it on a daily basis.

As usual John checked the Site N nest on the morning of 10 May. 5N(04), now more than halfway through incubation, was sitting tight on the eggs and 08(97) was away – presumably fishing. John decided to pop back later to check that all was well. When he did 08(97) was again absent and, worryingly, he was still not back by dark. After the events of the previous spring, this had an all too familiar ring to it. Next morning I was at the nest early but again there was no sign of 08(97). 5N(04) was resolutely sitting tight on the nest but we knew there was only so long she'd be able

to keep this up. During the incubation period males provide all of the fish for their mate and we knew that if we didn't intervene, 5N(04) would desert the nest to go fishing.

I phoned John Seaton, the Fishing Warden at the reservoir, and asked if he might be able to get hold of a fish or two for us. Always happy to help, John agreed to ask returning anglers if they'd be willing to donate their catch. The vast majority of anglers at the reservoir love seeing the Ospreys and we were hopeful that someone would help us out. Sure enough I got a call from John not long afterwards saying that he'd got a fish. Wanting to make sure that 5N(04) ate the fish John Wright and I collected a set of ladders and drove to Site N. I climbed up and placed the fish on the side of the nest away from the clutch of three eggs. We quickly retreated and watched. 5N(04) returned to the nest within minutes. She initially settled down to incubate, but stood up soon afterwards and began eating the fish. It was a warm day and with the sun high in the sky, the half hour that she was off the eggs while eating the fish wouldn't be a problem. The question was, what should we do next? 08(97) had now been absent for two days and it seemed certain he wasn't going to return. If we didn't intervene the nest was doomed to fail.

One thing was certain, we had to provide fish for 5N(04). Wanting to disturb her as little as possible we devised a feeding tray that we could position near the nest. Thanks to the wardens, we had a good supply of fish and by putting at least one fish on the tray each day we could guarantee that 5N(04) wouldn't go hungry. The problem was that if the weather took a turn for the worse and she got off

5N(04) on the feed tray erected at Site N following the disappearance of 08(97). It was hoped that providing fish for 5N(04) would encourage her to continue sitting on the eggs. She did so for several days before eventually deserting them. Once she had done so, they were incubated artificially.

09(98) intruding at Site B, April 2011. His repeated intrusions while 03(97) was away fishing resulted in two of the eggs not hatching. This sort of behaviour is common in Ospreys as a result of their semi-colonial nature.

the eggs to feed, the developing chicks might not survive. After discussing the problem with Roy Dennis and several farmer friends we decided that the best option would be to incubate the eggs artificially, ideally using a hen. After gaining the necessary permissions from Natural England, we got everything in place. On 20 May, 5N(04) left the nest at 7am and flew to the reservoir to bathe – leaving the eggs unattended for more than half an hour, and providing the first indication that she was less settled. Sure enough, she was on and off the eggs all morning, then stopped incubating in the afternoon. Although the sun was out, we had to act quickly. I climbed up to the nest, removed the eggs and replaced them with dummy ones to ensure that 5N(04) didn't think she had lost her clutch. We then took the eggs back to the reservoir and placed them under a broody hen, who was already sitting on a clutch of turkey eggs. It was then a question of waiting and hoping.

A week later, with hatching imminent, we checked the eggs. Sure enough, there were signs of life from at least one of them. Sadly, when we returned next morning, we found that the chick had died during hatching. This was not overly surprising; hatching is a difficult time for all young birds and there was every chance that this youngster had been weakened by the interrupted incubation. A day later we could hear tapping from the inside of one of the remaining eggs. This time rather than leaving it to hatch under the hen,

we moved it to Site O. AA(06) and his mate had raised three very good chicks there the previous summer and we were confident that AA(06) – now in his breeding prime – could provide sufficient fish to feed a family of four. Critically, the three Site O chicks were at exactly the same stage as 5N(04)'s brood. I climbed up to the nest to find two newly hatched chicks and an unhatched egg – perfect. I added the fourth chick and also placed a large trout on the side of the nest.

Although we felt confident that AA could raise all of the brood, we erected a feeding tray close to the nest so that we could supplement his fish deliveries. Two days later we returned to the nest and to our delight, found that all four eggs had hatched. Once again I left a large trout on the side of the nest.

After a week we decided to move the feeding tray to a better position, closer to the nest. I took the opportunity to check the progress of the chicks. I climbed the ladder hoping to find four healthy chicks. Instead I was greeted by the sight of one dead one. Although it was the same size as the remaining three youngsters and there was no obvious cause of death, the chances are that it had been out-competed by the other stronger chicks in the nest.

By now it had also become apparent that the third Site N egg was not going to hatch. When we checked it we found that it had died in the early stages of development – probably before 08(97) had gone missing. While this was all very

Two newly hatched chicks and two eggs in Site O nest, 24 May 2011.

Four chicks in Site O nest, 28 May 2011.

disappointing, on reflection we knew that we'd done all we could. Given the age of the chicks in the other nests, Site O was the only foster nest we could have used, and there is nothing to suggest that the chick that died would not have perished anyway. DNA tests would reveal whether the Site N chick was one of the three that survived. Interestingly, when we ringed the chicks in July we noted that one of the two males, ringed AZ(11), had a very white head that bore a remarkable resemblance to previous Site N chicks. So perhaps the foster chick had survived after all?

What the whole process did show was that artificial incubation is possible and that Ospreys will accept foster eggs and chicks. This is extremely valuable information that we will be able to use in future years at Rutland Water and elsewhere.

Of course none of this helped us to answer the question of what had happened to 08(97). Obviously even long-lived birds like Ospreys eventually die, but there was nothing in 08(97)'s behaviour leading up to his disappearance that suggested anything was wrong. What was worrying and extremely suspicious was that we knew he fished in the same areas as the two birds that had disappeared the previous spring. Despite extensive investigations by the local police, though, no information came to light.

It was clear that we needed to learn more about the birds' fishing habits and the only way we would be able to do that would be to satellite tag adult males. With that in mind we set up a public appeal in order to raise money to buy new GPS satellite transmitters.

We had the most incredible response. In less than a month we'd raised almost £6,000, enough to purchase two new transmitters to supplement the one we already had.

After 5N(04) abandoned her clutch of eggs at Site N – following the disappearance of her mate 08(97) – one of the clutch was moved to Site O where it hatched successfully. Although one juvenile in the nest failed to survive, the white head of one of the surviving chicks, AZ(11), suggested it was the individual that had been moved. All of 08(97)'s male offspring have shown similarly white head markings.

AA(06), who fledged from the Site B nest in 2006, returned to Rutland two years later without his ring. We ringed him again in 2011 when he was caught and satellite tagged. He was subsequently known as AW(06).

Having purchased the transmitters, now we needed to catch the birds. We decided we had best try and catch the males at the two nests where we had previously lost birds – Site O and Site N. Roy Dennis travelled from Scotland in mid-June and over the course of two days, using techniques Roy has refined over the years in Scotland, we caught and tagged AW(06) at Site O and 09(98), who had recently paired up with 5N(04), at Site N.

Having caught the two key males we could relax. We still had another transmitter to use so we drove to Site C, a vacant nest that 03(09) had visited the previous two evenings. Roy's recent satellite-tracking studies have shown that two-year-old Ospreys wander widely when they first return to the UK and it would have been great to catch 03(09), who fledged from the Site N nest in 2009. Sadly, though, the young male didn't appear. Nevertheless it had been a very good couple of days. The new GPS transmitters provide a location accurate to within a few metres every hour, so that for the first time we'd be able to monitor the fishing behaviour of the males in detail. Furthermore, should either bird go missing, we would know where.

Despite the disappearance of 08(97), 2011 proved to be another encouraging year, with ten chicks fledging from four successful nests. Among the ten young Rutland Ospreys who set out on migration in early September was a single chick from Site B. Over the years we've come to expect 03(97)

to raise two if not three chicks each year, but given events early in the spring at Site B, it was a relief that any young fledged successfully. The perils of semi-colonial nesting were highlighted early in the incubation period at Site B, when 09(98) – who at this stage of the season was still on his own – made repeated intrusions at the nest. These intrusions were far more aggressive than we had seen before and especially so when 03(97) was away fishing. On several successive mornings, 09(98) made repeated attempts to land on the nest, forcing the female – who had visited Site C regularly since she first bred with 03(97) in 2009 – to leave the eggs unattended in order to give chase. On one particularly cold morning, she left the eggs uncovered for at least 40 minutes. We feared that these intrusions would result in the nest failing completely, so it was a relief that one chick survived. Once 09(98) paired up with 5N(04), there were far fewer intrusions at Site B and the one chick – 33(10) – developed well. Within ten days of fledging 33(10) was venturing away from his nest for prolonged periods and even spent an afternoon on the Manton

09(98) after being fitted with a GPS solar-powered satellite transmitter. The transmitter provided a wealth of new information on his fishing habits in Rutland and migration to Senegal.

Bay nest where, despite the presence of three newly fledged juveniles, he was given a fish by 5R(04); a case of mistaken identity, we thought.

The Manton Bay nest is a great place to watch Osprey family life at any time of the year, but especially so in late summer. Two hides, Waderscrape and Shallow Water, offer superb views of the nest and once the juveniles are flying there can't be many better places to watch Ospreys in the UK. In 2011 three juveniles fledged from the nest and by late July all three were on the wing. Uneasy in the air at first, the youngsters quickly grew in confidence and by mid-August all three birds were making fishing attempts in the bay. The fact that the nest is surrounded by water certainly gives them ample opportunity to practise fishing before they set out on migration and their often comical attempts to catch fish make for entertaining viewing. The adult birds put on a good show too. 5R(04) often catches fish within sight of the hides and both adult birds regularly drop down to the water's edge to bathe. On other occasions they repeatedly dive into the water to cool down.

Perhaps the most encouraging aspect of the year was the fact that four of the nine birds that fledged in 2009 made it back. Of the four birds that returned – three males and one female – it was most poignant to see 03(09)

♂ 03(09) at Site C – 16·6·11   03(97) lives on!

2011 was a notable year due to the return of four of the nine chicks that had fledged from Rutland nests in 2009. One of them, 03(09), is the son of 08(97). He arrived three weeks after his father had disappeared in suspicious circumstances.

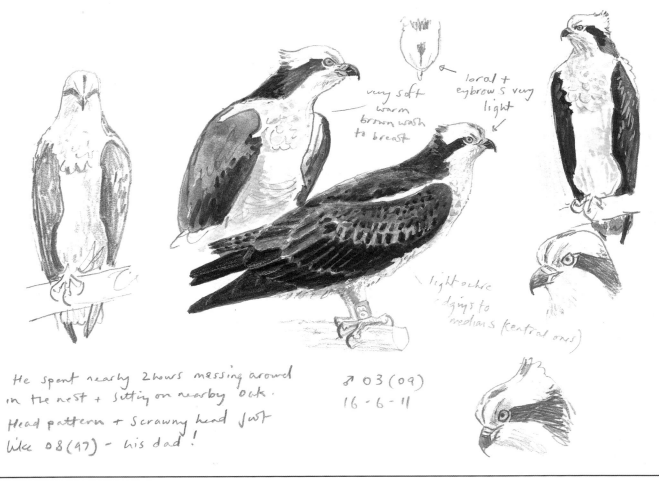

very soft warm brown wash to breast

loral + eybrow s very light

light ochre dings to medians (central ones)

He spent nearly 2 hours messing around in the nest + sitting on nearby oak. Head pattern + scrawny head just like 08(97) – his dad!

♂ 03(09) 16-6-11

06(09) on his return to Rutland Water, 10 June 2011. He was one of four 2009-fledged birds to return, and was also seen in Hampshire.

As is often the case with two-year-old returnees, all four birds made a brief visit to Rutland in late spring. They then made only sporadic appearances in June and July before becoming regular intruders at the breeding nests in August. From satellite-tracking studies we know that the youngsters explore far and wide during the first year back in the UK, and it was nice to be able to prove that this was the case for at least one of the 2009 contingent. After one brief visit to Rutland on 10 June, 06(09) disappeared for six weeks. During this time we had no idea how far afield he was exploring, but the mystery was solved when I received an email from Keith Betton, the Hampshire County recorder, in August. A colour-ringed Osprey had spent several weeks at a site just north of Southampton during the latter part of June and photographs showed that it was 06(09). So we now knew that after his brief visit to Rutland Water in June he had flown 120 miles south for six weeks, before returning to Rutland again later in the summer. The sighting again demonstrated the value of colour ringing, but also showed that the presence of the expanding Osprey colony in Rutland now had the potential to help Ospreys recolonise other parts of their former range. In 2009 I had been invited to travel down to Hampshire with Roy Dennis to talk about our work at Rutland Water and to encourage some of the local Hampshire conservationists to build artificial nests. I said during my talk at the meeting that because of the expanding population in Rutland there was every chance that artificial nests would be used by Rutland birds – and 06(09)'s time in Hampshire backed that up.

back in Rutland. He returned a few weeks after his father, 08(97), had disappeared and it would be a wonderful legacy to see him breeding in the area in years to come. His return certainly proved what we had first thought in 2009; he was a strong bird.

AZ(11) knocks his parents off their perch after making his first flight at Site O, July 2011. Landing is often the most difficult aspect of any young Osprey's first flight.

2012

An increasingly familiar sound at the Osprey nests in Rutland is the plaintive 'chip' call given by the breeding birds when an intruding Osprey appears over their nest. It was a sound we got very used to hearing in 2012.

In late May or early June, young two-year-old Ospreys start to return to the UK for the first time. They are on a reconnaissance mission – most Ospreys don't breed until they are three or four years old, and this means that young birds have at least one or two summers in the UK before settling down at a nest. This is a crucial period for them because it provides an opportunity to scout out potential nest sites. It's clear that young Ospreys prefer to take over an established territory rather than to build their own nest from scratch, so the birds spend their first few summers back in the UK wandering over a large area in search of somewhere to breed. The six weeks that 06(09) had spent in Hampshire the previous summer had shown how far the Rutland birds might be exploring. Events in 2012 were even more revealing.

Surprisingly, one of the first Ospreys to return to Rutland in spring 2012 was 00(09). Now three years old, we had only seen the young female twice the previous summer, but her arrival on 23 March signalled a clear intention to breed. She initially joined 5R(04) – who had also returned earlier than ever – at the Manton Bay nest. It is not unusual to see a young bird attempting to oust an older one at an established nest, but 00(09) was no match for 5R(04)'s regular mate when she returned a few days later. Unperturbed, 00(09) continued to visit the established nest sites in search of a mate. Sadly, however, there were no unpaired males of breeding age – the first time we had had an excess of females – and by early May she began to wander over a wider area. She spent three days at Carsington Water in Derbyshire between 19 and 21 May then, four days later, intruded at the Cors Dyfi nest in Mid Wales where another Rutland bird, 03(08), was breeding for a second year. A few weeks later she was back in Rutland, but it was now clear that her search for a mate could take her anywhere in southern Britain. And she wasn't the only one. Four days before 00(09) had intruded at Cors Dyfi, the high-definition nest cameras there had helped identify another Rutland bird, 12(10). Unlike 00(09), 12(10) hadn't been seen in Rutland, but it was encouraging to know she was back in the UK. As it turned out she spent most of her summer in Wales, making only one brief visit to Rutland, on 23 July, before returning to the Dyfi Estuary. It was fascinating to be able to chart these cross-country movements, which again demonstrated the potential for the Rutland birds to breed anywhere in the south of the UK.

More exciting news arrived in mid-May when we received an email from Roger Haggar. Roger had photographed a

00(09) spent the summer in Rutland but also visited the Cors Dyfi nest – satellite-tracking studies and colour-ring sightings have shown that young birds wander widely when they first return to the UK.

blue-ringed female Osprey at Arlington Reservoir in Sussex. It wasn't possible to read the inscription on the ring in Roger's initial photos, but later shots showed that he had seen another of the 2010 contingent, 24(10). She remained on the south coast for much of the summer, and although we didn't see her in Rutland, we suspect that she made at least one brief visit – just as 12(10) had done – at some point.

12(10) and 24(10) may have spent their summers elsewhere, but 2012 was notable for the number of non-breeding birds that were present in Rutland. In addition to 00(09), the three other three-year-old birds that we had first identified in 2011 all returned. 01(09), 03(09) and 06(09) were all present from mid-May onwards and, by late summer, both 01(09) and 03(09) had established territories, 03(09) at Site O, where he paired up with the metal-ringed Scottish female who had previously raised young with 06(00) and AW(06). Sadly, satellite-tracking data had shown that AW(06) was killed in the Ivory Coast over the winter. Three 2010-fledged males – 11(10), 28(10) and 30(10) – and another 2010-fledged female – 25(10) – also made it back, making 2012 easily the most successful

03(09) with metal-ringed female on the Site O nest. 03(09) took over the territory when AW(06) failed to return from migration.

year in terms of new returnees. In all, ten of the 22 birds that fledged in 2009/10 had made it back, an extremely encouraging return rate. By late summer intruding Ospreys had become a regular sight at all the breeding nests, with up to five or six birds sometimes intruding en masse. It made for spectacular viewing for anyone lucky enough to be there to witness it.

Apart from the number of returning young birds, 2012 was also notable for the weather. Due to heavy rain on and off throughout the summer the reservoir reached its highest ever level and made life extremely difficult for breeding birds. But fortunately for the Ospreys, hatching coincided with a rare spell of warm sunny weather. 5R(04) and his unringed mate wowed the crowds in Manton Bay again, raising two chicks that were watched online via the webcam by up to 5,000 people a day. 03(97) bred for the twelfth successive year, raising three chicks at Site B with the same unringed female as in the previous three years; 08(01) and 30(05) produced another two chicks at Site K; and, perhaps most significantly of all, 09(98) bred for the first time, raising two male chicks with 5N(04). At 14 years old he was the oldest first-time breeder in the Rutland colony, and probably anywhere in the UK. Evidence, if it were needed, that perseverance can pay off.

Thanks to the dedication of our 160-strong volunteer team, we monitor the various breeding nests in Rutland from dawn until dusk on most days. This is especially important at certain stages of the breeding season, in particular at fledging. And fledging this year proved more problematic for

the young birds than ever before. All three of the juveniles at Site B ended up on the ground at one point or another: 2F was brought down by a strong gust of wind, crash-landing in a dense patch of nettles, and 1F was found by volunteer Mick Ward, on the ground and completely waterlogged after a day of torrential rain. Fortunately we were able to rescue both birds and get them back into the air again. 3F, meanwhile,

09(98) with his family at Site N. At 14 years he was very old for a first-time breeder.

03(97) arriving back at Site B on 19 March 2012. He is always one of the first birds to return each spring.

disappeared for more than 24 hours, before eventually reappearing covered in mud; she too had obviously been brought down by the bad weather.

Events at Site B, though, turned out to be nothing more than a prelude to what happened in Manton Bay. Of the two juveniles, the male, ringed 8F, was the more advanced. He made his maiden flight on 16 July, five days before his sister, 9F. When 9F finally plucked up the courage to leave the nest, she completed a short circuit of the bay before attempting to land next to her father, who was eating a fish on one of the artificial T-perches nearby. All she succeeded in doing, however, was to knock him off the perch. 5R(04) – who hadn't watched 9F leave the nest – was clearly surprised by this and, after taking the fish to the nest, dive-bombed his daughter, knocking her off the perch then down into the long grass at the water's edge. Fortunately volunteers Sue Walton and Doreen Thompson had seen exactly where she had landed so John Wright and I were able to go down to the bay and pick her up.

Our initial plan was to release her straightaway, but before we had a chance to do that we noticed a wound on her right wing, presumably caused by 5R's attack. The wound was a nasty one, so we took her to the Oakham Veterinary Hospital where vet Luke Knowles examined her. Fortunately Luke was able to stitch up the wound with the loss of only one secondary feather.

Having been given the all-clear, we headed to the south shore of Manton Bay to release 9F. I launched her into the air

and, as we hoped, she flew away from us and towards the nest. But then she suddenly changed direction and headed off south-west towards Manton village. To make matters worse she was chased first by a Buzzard, and then again by 5R. We lost her behind the trees, fearing the worst. Fortunately, though, after a search of the sheep fields close to the village, we found her perched on the ground. We approached slowly and picked her up again. It was clear that releasing her for a second time was not an option so instead we kept her overnight.

Next morning we decided that rather than risking another failed release, our best option was to put the young female directly back on the nest. Getting to the Manton Bay nest isn't easy – it requires a boat and triple-extending ladders – but it was worth it. Once I had placed 9F back on the nest, she crouched down and remained there all day. Mission accomplished.

Not that the drama ended there. By next morning 9F was flying well, but was being chased by her father every time she took to the air. His behaviour was almost inexplicable and certainly unprecedented, but the only possible explanation was that, having been knocked off the T-perch by his daughter, 5R(04) still perceived her as a threat. The chasing continued for several more extremely worrying days, before he finally relented.

Within two weeks, 9F was back on track and making long exploratory flights away from the nest. Like the two chicks we rescued at Site B, it would be marvellous to see her return in 2014 – more birds to help swell an already expanding colony.

1F shortly after he was ringed at Site B. A few days later he had to be rescued having been grounded by a day of heavy rain shortly after his first flight.

Volunteer Diary, Lynda Berry, 2009

Rush Hour at Site N – Wednesday 8 July

I love being a volunteer for the Osprey project and consider myself very lucky to be allowed to watch over these magnificent birds that never cease to fascinate. Another added bonus is that the other volunteers are a great bunch of people from different walks of life and of all ages, one of whom is Christine. I met Christine earlier this year at the first Family Osprey Fun Day at Lyndon and we got on well. At the second Fun Day she asked if she could join me on one of my shifts at Site N as she hadn't visited it yet. Sure enough she telephoned this week and I arranged to pick her up.

After the heatwave last week, I was disappointed to see that it was raining and the forecast for the day was not good. Thinking that as volunteers we would never say, 'I don't want to come today, it's raining,' I called her to suggest that she might like to come another day when the weather was better; the walk to the hide is very muddy and you can get drenched from the long grass and over-reaching crops, but she assured me that it would be OK.

The previous evening Tim Mackrill had called me to say that at some time the farmer would be fence mending in the field surrounding the nest and that if I was concerned about the adult Ospreys being disturbed too much, I should let him know. Sure enough, soon after 9am both began alarm-calling. I was convinced that the farmer must be arriving, but before he came into view we realised it was three intruding Ospreys that were the main problem. The two chicks on the nest were well hunkered down as their parents called to them. I put in a quick call to Tim to let him know the situation and he said he would come over a little later. The intruding Ospreys were persistent and the scene carried on for an hour, with all four – or was it five – birds up in the air on several occasions. We made a few observations of the intruders – one had the eighth primary missing in each wing, one had a very white breast and one had the broader wings of a female – were our eyes playing tricks? Where's John Wright when you really need him? Christine was later to remark to Tim that they had sometimes been so close you felt you could reach out and touch them.

Eventually Tim and Diana Spencer arrived with new stools for the hide, a replacement scope and monitoring sheets. They stayed with us for over an hour and Tim's trained eye told us that we had 09(98) and 32(05) around. We all marvelled at how extraordinary it was for us to be watching this spectacle in England.

Peter and Di arrived as our replacements after Tim and Diana had left and we discovered that once again five birds were in the air. Christine's and my observation that one of our intruders was a female was soon confirmed when she landed on a pylon with a male in hot pursuit and mating was attempted.

We left Peter and Di to carry on watching over these precious birds and their offspring. Sometimes I love the solitude of doing a shift alone, absorbing everything going on around me, but this morning I was so pleased to share the experience with Christine; it just wouldn't have been the same on my own. Somehow these birds eat into your very soul; I'm just off now to find out if 03 has returned to Site B as we heard over the radio that he had been missing for four or five hours this morning. I'm then going have a large G&T.

Site N – 20/6/09

Fishing Ospreys at Rutland Water

A SUPREME PREDATOR

There is no doubt that one of the reasons why Ospreys have become so well known in the UK over the past 60 years is the fact that they are such impressive birds – watching one pluck a fish out of the water is not an easy sight to forget. One of the privileges of being involved with the Rutland Osprey Project is being able to watch them doing it every day.

Rutland Water was considered an excellent place for the translocation project because it has such an abundant supply of fish. The reservoir has quickly established itself as one of the top fly-fishing venues in the country and Anglian Water stock it with around 100,000 trout every year. Add to that around 20 or so other naturally occurring species, and it's not hard to understand why this is such a good place for Ospreys.

Ospreys are extremely well adapted for fishing. They have to be – they are the only bird of prey that feeds exclusively on fish in the UK. Although there are odd anecdotal stories of Ospreys catching other prey, fish generally make up 100% of their diet. Of the various adaptations the birds have evolved in order to catch their prey, two are particularly notable. The first is their eyes. Their outstanding vision allows them to spot fish from 100 metres or more above the water. At Rutland Water fishing Ospreys usually drift slowly across the reservoir, often for between 30 and 100 metres, looking

5R(04) fishing at Rutland Water.

1. An adult Osprey at the start of a dive. Having caught sight of a fish, a hunting Osprey folds its wings and dives arrow-like towards the water.

2. At the last minute the Osprey thrusts its feet forwards until they are just in front of its head. At the same time it extends its toes, ready to make the strike.

3. The Osprey crashes into the water, striking the fish with its outstretched talons. Fish are taken either from the water's surface, or just below it. The birds' razor-sharp claws and scaly feet help them to grip hold of the fish.

4. Once the Osprey has made contact with the fish it manoeuvres it underwater using its specially adapted zygodactylic (opposable) toes to ensure that the fish is facing forwards as it leaves the water. Sometimes the fish are so heavy that fishing Ospreys have to make several attempts to take off from the water's surface. This process is made all the harder as the fish are almost always still alive and trying desperately to escape; it is not uncommon to see Ospreys drop fish as they attempt to pull them out of the water.

5. Once the Osprey has a firm grip on the fish, the bird flies off with its catch, carrying the fish headfirst, torpedo-like, to reduce wind resistance. Satellite tracking has revealed that some of the Rutland Water birds have caught fish up to 15 miles from their nest site.

for signs of movement. A sure sign that a bird has seen a fish occurs when it stops and hovers over one particular spot, its eyes fixed on the water's surface.

Ospreys often stoop a few feet then hover again, sometimes repeating the process until they are less than 15 metres above the water. Then, suddenly, they fold their wings and dive, arrow-like, towards the water. On other occasions they dive almost without warning from a much greater height – dives like this are a spectacular sight. As they dive towards the water in a seemingly effortless manoeuvre, the birds thrust their talons forwards, stretching out their four toes to their full extent. Each toe has a razor-sharp claw and a scaly underside, giving the bird maximum grip. By the time the bird hits the water the talons are directly in front of its head, ensuring that it does not lose sight of the fish at the vital moment.

Sometimes the birds pluck a fish effortlessly from the surface of the water, barely making a ripple, but more often than not they crash into the water, sending up a great splash and temporarily disappearing from view. It's usually possible to tell if they've caught a fish because it takes them some time to take off from the water; they must make sure they have a firm grip on the fish before they attempt to fly off. As they take off you sometimes see them manoeuvring the fish into the characteristic torpedo position. It's here that a special zygodactylic adaptation – the ability to reverse one of their forward-facing toes – really comes into its own. Having grabbed hold of the fish a reversible toe enables a bird to manoeuvre the fish into the most aerodynamic position – head first. It then heads off to its nest site or a favoured perch with the fish still very much alive, struggling to free itself.

♂ 03 (97) hit the water 17 times during 2 hrs of nonStop fishing. At one point he got hold of a very large Trout but while trying to get a grip of it a Cormorant flew in, dived under the water and stole it from his talons.

A PRIVILEGED VIEW

Over the years we've been treated to some truly spectacular views of fishing Ospreys at Rutland Water. Of all the successful dives I've seen, perhaps the most memorable came in 2011. Volunteers Barrie Galpin and Ken Davies were doing their regular stint in Waderscrape Hide on a Sunday afternoon and radioed us at the Lyndon Visitor Centre not long after they'd arrived to say that 5R(04) had left the nest and was heading our way. Just as 5R(04) came into view he folded his wings in characteristic style and crashed into the water. We immediately knew that he'd caught a fish because he was floundering around, evidently in an effort to keep hold of the fish, which at that point remained out of sight. The birds sometimes remain on the water with their wings spreadeagled for half a minute or more as they grapple with the fish and that's exactly what 5R(04) did. It seemed to take an age for him to attempt to lift his quarry out of the water. As he did so, we got a quick flash of what was clearly a very large silvery fish. It was so big that despite repeated attempts to take off, 5R(04) couldn't muster the strength to lift it out of the water. After five or more failed attempts to take off, 5R(04) settled for a different tactic. Using his wings like oars, he paddled his way to shore, a 'swim' of more than 10 metres. When he finally reached land, he dragged the fish out of the water, revealing an enormous Bream that must have weighed nearly 1.5kg. Despite constant hassle from a pair of Carrion Crows, he was finally able to tuck into his meal. More than an hour later, he'd just about devoured the head and was able to take the huge fish back to the nest. Even without the head, the fish looked enormous as 5R(04) delivered it to his waiting mate on the nest. It certainly drew gasps of amazement from the assembled onlookers who were watching events unfold on the big screen at the Lyndon Visitor Centre. Later that day I posted the clip on YouTube and it remains our most popular video.

Over the past decade we've built up a comprehensive knowledge of the birds' fishing behaviour at Rutland Water and elsewhere in the area. From data collected at nests by our large and extremely dedicated volunteer team, combined with observations around the reservoir, we know just about everything there is to know about fishing Ospreys in Rutland.

When the birds first began breeding, we organised coordinated fishing watches amongst volunteers. Around a dozen of us would station ourselves around the reservoir either at first light or in the late afternoon, in an effort to record where the birds were fishing and, hopefully, to identify new territories of young birds. It was great fun. Each observer was given a radio, enabling us to 'hand over' Ospreys as they flew around the reservoir. For three

08(97) delivering a large Bream to the Manton Bay nest in June 2007.

or four hours, we would know the exact movements of each individual. Sometimes the birds would catch fish very quickly, while at other times it took them much longer. On one early-morning watch 03(97) made 17 unsuccessful dives in two hours of fishing before he finally caught something. At one point he actually got hold of a fish, but as he grappled with it, a Cormorant stole it from below the surface. We regularly see Lesser and Great Black-backed Gulls hassling Ospreys in an effort to make them drop their fish, but that remains the only occasion we've seen a Cormorant actually rob an Osprey of its meal.

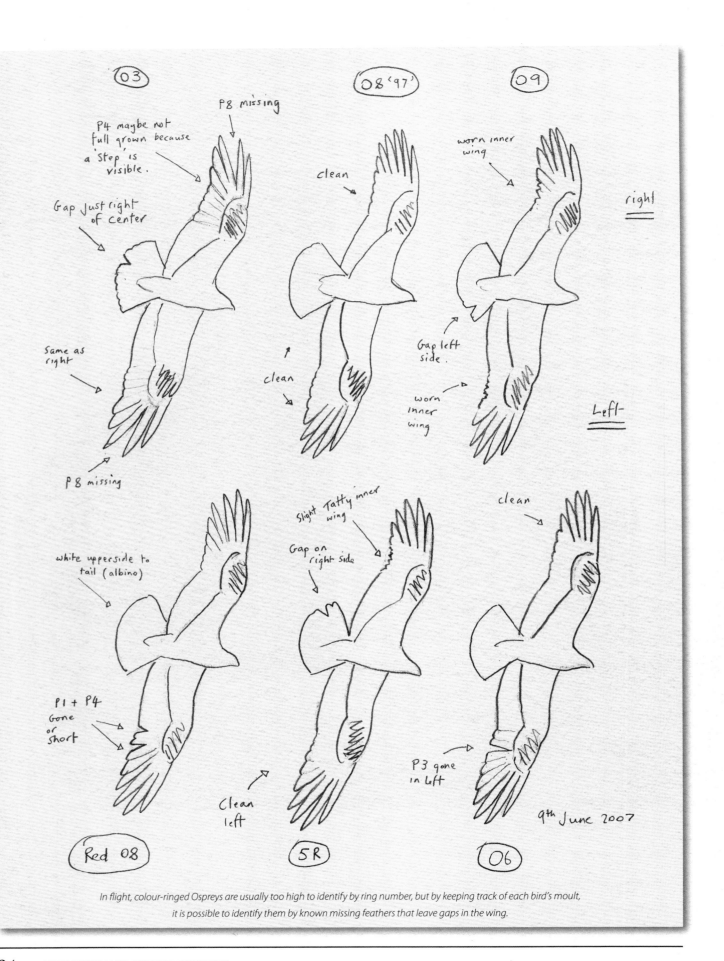

In flight, colour-ringed Ospreys are usually too high to identify by ring number, but by keeping track of each bird's moult,
it is possible to identify them by known missing feathers that leave gaps in the wing.

OSPREYS AS INDIVIDUALS

One of the real challenges during coordinated watches was identifying individual birds while they were fishing. In recent years the advent of digital photography has made identifying colour-ringed birds in flight a relatively simple task. By zooming in on a photograph, it's often possible to read the two-digit inscription in the ring. This, however, is not the only way. Over the past decade, we – and John Wright, in particular – have used various other methods to identify individual birds. The first is by the moult. During the course of the year Ospreys continuously moult their feathers, and although this goes largely unnoticed to the untrained eye, observing the moult is an excellent method of keeping track of who's who. Primary feathers – the ten large flight feathers on the end of a bird's wings – are particularly obvious when they're moulted. A telltale gap in the wing betrays the fact that a bird has moulted a primary feather and because it takes several weeks for the new feather to grow, this gap remains prominent for a fairly long time. It's rare for two birds to be in the same stage of moult at any one time, so once you've established which birds have which gaps, it's a fairly simple task to identify them when they fly overhead.

A second method that John has used very effectively recently to identify birds in flight, is by their underwing markings. Ospreys have beautifully marked underwings, with distinctive brown spots and streaks on their carpals. By comparing his photos of the carpal patterns of individual Ospreys from year to year, John has been able to show that these markings are unique to each bird, and more significantly, do not vary from year to year. In many ways they're the same as human fingerprints. This technique has proved especially useful when comparing the many unringed female Ospreys who pass through Rutland each year. As already discussed elsewhere, female Ospreys have been shown to be less site-faithful than males and, to date, three unringed and one Scottish-ringed female have raised young in the Rutland Water area. We've also identified numerous other unringed birds, some of which stay for a few days, while others – such as the one who summered in 2005 – stay for much longer. By comparing his photos of newly arrived females with ones taken in previous years, John is quickly able to establish whether a bird has visited before. An excellent example came in 2009. In late March, John and I were sitting in Shallow Water Hide when an unringed female appeared from the south and alighted briefly on the nest. After a few minutes she took off, circled higher and higher until she was nothing more than a dot in the sky, then headed purposefully north to resume – or so we thought – her spring migration. Having seen this we were convinced that she was a passing migrant, but three days later, when a female joined 03(97) at Site B, John's underwing photos revealed that it was the Manton Bay bird. We hadn't seen her in the intervening period, so who knows where else she had visited, but it was great to be able to prove that it was the same bird. What's more, she stayed to breed and John was later able to show that she had intruded at the Site B nest several times the previous summer. It's this kind of information that we can normally only glean from colour-ringed birds, so John's underwing technique is invaluable in helping us understand how the colony is developing.

Unringed female intruding at Site B on 20 July 2008 – she returned next year to breed.

Unringed female at Site B, 7 April 2009. By comparing photographs of her underwing pattern with previous photos, John Wright was able to confirm that she was a female he had photographed intruding at Site B the previous year and at Manton Bay on 29 March.

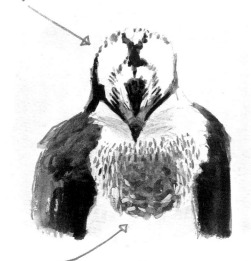

female

very strong crown pattern

Solid centre to breast with streaks across top and sides

Male 5R

weaker crown pattern

Softer brown breast without strong streaks

The above illustrations show the Manton Bay breeding pair and its diagnostic plumage features. The female has a distinctive crown pattern which makes it easy to identify her each year.

♂ 05 (08)
5·8·10

small nick in P6

P3 full grown

P2 almost full grown

large Gap

Right

P2 new + full grown

P3 almost full grown

chunk out of P6

These sketches show adult males at differing stages of moult.

♂ 09
8·7·10

P7 ¾ grown in right

gap just off center

P7 gone in left

The final identification technique – not so good when the birds are in flight, but useful when they're perched – is recognition by head patterns. Like their underwings, Ospreys' head markings are unique to each individual and don't appear to change over time. All Ospreys have the characteristic dark brown 'highwayman's mask' through their eye, as well as a striking broad central streak that runs from the forehead up onto their crown. Most also have dark 'eyebrows' and numerous other dark streaks and spots that contrast with the rest of their predominantly white heads. Some females are very heavily marked and, at the opposite end of the spectrum, there are males – including one or two Rutland birds – that have much whiter heads. This gives some individuals a classic, very clean-cut appearance, while others look much more messy. The problem, especially compared with the underwing technique, is that some of the streaks are only visible at close range. If you get a close view of an Osprey, it can appear very different from how it looks when viewed over a much greater distance. We're always wary, therefore, when identifying birds purely by their head patterns. Having said this, there are some individuals that are so distinctive that the identification can be guaranteed. One such bird is the unringed female who 5R(04) first bred with in 2010. Aside from three very strong, clean streaks on her forehead, she has brown markings on the crown of her head that form a cross. There is no other bird in the Rutland population quite like it and that makes her easy to identify each spring. All we need her to do when she arrives at her nest is to lean forwards. The high-definition camera that we installed at the nest in 2012 makes identifying her even easier.

Breast markings can be important too. In general, female Ospreys have a much heavier, more well-defined breast-band than males but, as ever, there are variations. 5R(04), for instance, is very well marked for a male, whereas 03(97) has a much cleaner, whiter breast. Like head patterns, breast-bands can be distinctive, but the amount of visible streaking also varies greatly with distance and it's usually a combination of the three characteristics – underwing markings, head patterns and breast markings – that helps to clinch the identification of a certain individual. This has certainly been the case at Site B, where 03(97) nearly always attracts an unringed female to his nest before the arrival of his regular mate each spring. Over the years we've become well accustomed to females – usually unringed – joining a male at a nest for a day or so each March. These females are invariably birds that already have an established nest further north, and are stopping off with a male in Rutland for nothing more than a free meal. Perhaps it says something about Site B, or perhaps 03(97) himself, that it's usually him who attracts these females each year. A quick count of unringed females John has identified at Site B in previous springs suggests that as many as ten different birds may have taken advantage of 03(97) in this way. 08(97) also attracted his fair share of passing Scottish females, especially before pairing up with 5N(04) in 2006.

A CHANGING CATCH

Having come up with various techniques to identify individual Ospreys, we've also become well practised at fish identification, enabling us to build up a comprehensive picture of the foraging habits of the birds. In 2003 I carried out the fieldwork for my undergraduate dissertation on Osprey foraging behaviour. The first part of the study was based in Scotland, but I spent the latter part of the summer watching Ospreys fishing at Rutland Water. The idea was to understand what factors most influence Osprey foraging success, and in order to do that I needed to watch the birds in action. Not exactly a bad way to spend a few months. One of my abiding memories of that summer was sitting between Normanton Church and the dam, watching Ospreys catching Roach. The Roach were congregating in large shoals close to the surface, and they made easy pickings for the fishing Ospreys. The shoals were so big that it was sometimes possible to see them from the shoreline, and as the birds dived into the water, the fish could be seen diving to safety. It certainly made for spectacular viewing, and more importantly for the Ospreys, very easy fishing. On still evenings with little wind and a bit of cloud cover – ideal conditions for foraging Ospreys – I would see three or more birds catching fish in front of me. It was as predictable as it was enjoyable.

The observations made by the volunteers monitoring Site B that year and in the next few summers backed up my observations. Of the 400 or so fish the volunteers recorded 03(97) delivering to the Site B nest each summer, around half were Roach. At this point it's important to bear in mind that, during the breeding season, male and female Ospreys have very clearly defined roles. If a female Osprey has a good mate then she shouldn't have to fish for herself from the day she arrives back from migration until her young are flying in late July or early August; it is the male's job to catch fish for his family. This has been true every year at Site B, where apart from one or two exceptions 03(97) has proved an expert provider for his family. He greets his returning mate with a freshly caught Roach or trout, then continues to provide fish for her for the rest of the summer. By monitoring the nest from dawn until dusk virtually every day since 03(97) first bred at Site B in 2001, we've been able to build up a very comprehensive picture of his daily routine, and significantly, the fish he has caught. Despite the fact that the Site B shed – our monitoring post for more than a decade – is positioned 300 metres from the nest, it's surprisingly easy to identify the fish he brings back for his mate. Once back somewhere near the nest, 03(97) usually tucks into the head of the fish before taking the remainder up to his mate on the nest. This gives the observers positioned in the shed the opportunity to identify the fish – which is often in the final throes of life and still kicking in a last desperate attempt to free itself from

03(97) with a pike at Site B, 4 April 2005. Pike are often one of the first fish to be caught by the newly arrived Ospreys each spring.

03(97) with a Roach at Site B, 8 June 2009. Round-the-clock monitoring of the Site B nest has indicated that the population of Roach in the reservoir may have declined in recent years.

the Osprey's well-adapted talons. Using high-quality optics, on maximum magnification, it's relatively straightforward to separate the half a dozen or so species that 03(97) regularly catches. You quickly pick up the fact that trout are silvery with a flat tail, while Roach have a reddish forked tail. The other regular fish – Perch, pike, Bream and Rudd – are all sufficiently different for our observations to have a high degree of accuracy. It is certainly as accurate as you can hope to be when you're 300 metres from the fish. As I was seeing at the reservoir, Roach were by far the most numerous species brought back to the nest by 03(97). Observations by volunteers showed that in 2004, 03(97) brought back three times as many Roach as trout. Despite the fact that Anglian Water stock the reservoir with so many trout every year, Roach were probably more numerous and, significantly, easier to catch. The large shoals at the eastern end of the reservoir clearly made life very easy for the Ospreys.

In recent years, things have changed. The value of long-term monitoring has been demonstrated by our findings at Site B and the other nests monitored round the clock by the project's volunteers. In 2007 the data collected at Site B showed that, for the first time, 03(97) caught more trout than Roach. Not only this, but it seemed that fishing in the reservoir had become more difficult for the birds. Whereas a few years previously – such as the summer I was carrying out the fieldwork for my dissertation – the shoals of Roach had proved easy pickings, now the birds appeared to be having to work harder for their fish. So what had changed? Anecdotal evidence – including our own – suggested that the big shoals of Roach simply weren't there. While we were out on the reservoir on our Osprey cruises it was becoming noticeable

that the areas the birds favoured for fishing were changing – and were now much less predictable. Fishermen too were noticing a difference. They were not reporting the big shoals of Roach that used to be so common. The Osprey population was far too small for it to have any significant effect on the stocks, so perhaps another predator was having an impact? Cormorants are a direct competitor with the Ospreys for fish and with a breeding population of more than 80 pairs at the reservoir, they may well have contributed to the decline. They were not the only suspects. Zander, a fish on the increase at Rutland Water and various other sites around the country, are likely to predate Roach fry – preventing individuals reaching a size where they could be taken by the Ospreys. Whatever the root cause, it was obvious that Roach had declined and that this was having an impact on the birds' fishing habits.

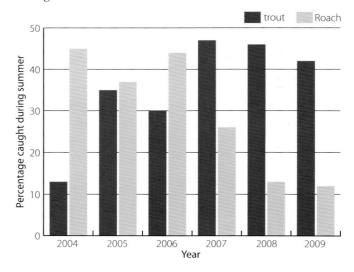

DAILY ROUTINES

Rutland Water will inevitably remain the most important foraging site for birds in the colony, but the decline in Roach numbers has triggered an undoubted shift in the birds' fishing habits. While 03(97) and his compatriots still fish in the reservoir each day, over the last few years they have begun to wander further afield during fishing trips. Prior to the summer of 2011 we knew that they visited numerous smaller lakes and ponds in the area, especially when the weather made fishing difficult in the main reservoir, but once we had satellite tagged two birds – 09(98) and AW(06) – we were able to build up a much more comprehensive picture of their daily movements. 09(98) was translocated to Rutland Water in 1998 and first returned there two years later. For the next 11 summers he became something of a perennial bachelor, holding territory at various sites around Rutland without ever breeding successfully. Then, when 08(97) disappeared in spring 2011, 09(98) paired up with 5N(04) at Site N before finally raising two chicks in 2012. Having

seen 09(98) fishing away from Rutland Water on numerous occasions we were keen to catch him and satellite tag him in order to follow his daily movements. We already knew that he fished various lakes and ponds around Rutland – making regular visits to a small lake next to the 18th green at Greetham Valley Golf Course, among others – but by fitting him with a satellite transmitter we would be able to follow his daily movements in unprecedented detail. We were delighted, therefore, when we caught and tagged him on 18 June 2011.

The results confirmed our suspicions. Although 09(98) visited Rutland Water most days, generally favouring the eastern end of the reservoir for fishing, he also visited many other lakes in the area. By the end of the summer he'd visited just about every corner of Rutland, and regularly fished at Eyebrook Reservoir as well as Rutland Water.

AW(06) provided us with more interesting information. Like 09(98), he generally favoured the Rutland reservoirs for fishing, but he also made 30-mile round trips to Naseby and Hollowell Reservoirs in Northamptonshire at least once a week. Roy Dennis has recorded similar movements by

09(98) after being fitted with a satellite transmitter, 18 June 2011. The transmitter revealed that, although he favoured Rutland Water for fishing, he also visited a range of other water bodies in the area.

08(97) being hassled by Jackdaws while he tries to eat a Trout. 15-20hr
14-5-09.

his satellite-tagged adult birds in north-east Scotland, but it was fascinating to see one of our own birds venturing so far afield, particularly as he had an apparently abundant supply of fish much closer to home. Presumably the Northamptonshire reservoirs are places that AW(06) visited as a two-year-old – we know young birds wander large distances when they first return to the UK – and perhaps he went to them when fishing at Rutland Water and Eyebrook was difficult. One noticeable difference between 09(98) and AW(06) during summer 2011 was that 09(98) was a more regular visitor to small lakes and ponds. Although this could be attributable to the fact that 09(98) wasn't breeding and was therefore free to explore a larger area, his greater experience and knowledge of fishing sites was probably important too. 2011 was 09(98)'s twelfth summer in Rutland and since he first returned in 2000 he will have developed a comprehensive knowledge of all the water bodies in the area; certainly more so than AW(06), who was seven years his junior. It's inevitable that over the course of an Osprey's lifetime it discovers new fishing sites. This is certainly true of 03(97). In his first few years of breeding at Site B, when we regularly carried out coordinated watches around Rutland Water, he rarely ventured anywhere other than the reservoir for his fish. Now he's a regular visitor to one of the local trout farms – ironically the same one that we got all our fish for the translocation from – and also two small lakes situated 5 miles from his nest site. Although the fish 03(97) catches

at these sites are rarely as big as the reservoir ones, they are almost certainly easier to come by. This change in behaviour may initially have been prompted by the decline in Roach, but it's a shift that is probably typical of most Ospreys as they become older and more experienced.

There is undoubtedly some variation between birds; some, like 09(98), are probably just bolder than others. Unfortunately this isn't necessarily a good trait. Whereas the vast majority of landowners in Rutland are delighted to see Ospreys fishing in their lakes, the disappearance of three birds – 06(00), 32(05) and 08(97) – after their return from migration was a worrying trend. 32(05), in particular, was always very bold – sometimes fishing less than 10 metres away from onlookers and ultimately this may have resulted in his demise. Sadly it seems that as Ospreys spread through England, persecution will remain an issue in some places. While most people will enjoy seeing these majestic birds back in areas where they were once common, there will be some sites where they are not welcomed. Our evidence, however, suggests that fishing Ospreys have very little impact on fish stocks. Although a breeding male needs to catch up to five fish a day at the height of the breeding season, our satellite-tracking data show that these fish are taken from a number of different sites. In 2012, when 09(98) was breeding for the first time, he rarely visited the same site on successive fishing trips. Whereas some species – like Cormorants – can clear a pond of fish, this is not the case with Ospreys. Furthermore, Ospreys will only ever nest in low densities. Roy Dennis's research in Scotland suggests that loose colonies of 10–15 pairs will become the norm in England. These colonies are likely to be centred around suitable fishing sites – such as Rutland Water and Eyebrook Reservoir – and birds in these areas will inevitably visit smaller lakes and ponds too. In such low densities they're unlikely to have a negative impact. And even when they do cause problems, there are always novel solutions. In Aviemore in northern Scotland, wildlife photographers pay significant sums of money to spend a few hours photographing fishing Ospreys at Rothiemurchus Fish Farm. Several years ago the owners of the fish farm, realising that they were unlikely to be able to stop the Ospreys taking their trout, made the forward-thinking decision to allow birdwatchers to come in and enjoy the spectacle at very close range. Now, the advent of digital photography has made the Ospreys an even more lucrative source of income for the fish farm. As Ospreys become more common in England, owners of coarse fishing lakes and trout farms may be persuaded to do the same. It certainly seems a sustainable way forward.

THE RUTLAND HIERARCHY

It's not just the weather, experience and fish populations that dictate a male Osprey's fishing routines – the actions of other Ospreys also have an influence. In Scotland and elsewhere, various studies have shown that at the best fishing grounds a clear hierarchy exists between individual Ospreys. Due to their tendency to nest in loose colonies, close to other Ospreys, the birds sometimes find themselves fishing together. In the years when Roach were numerous at Rutland Water and fishing was very straightforward for the birds, it was sometimes possible to see three birds fishing in the same corner of the reservoir. However, as fishing has become more difficult at the reservoir, a clearer hierarchy seems to have developed. The older, more experienced birds – 03(97) and 09(98), for example – are the most dominant and they often chase younger birds away from their favoured fishing spots. 09(98), for instance, went through a period when he didn't let any other Ospreys – 03(97) aside – fish in the North Arm of Rutland Water. Although he had an established territory away from the reservoir, once it was clear that he wasn't going to attract a mate in time to breed, he spent increasing amounts of time perched close to Tim Appleton's cottage at Burley Fishponds. If another Osprey approached, he would give the distinctive intruder 'chip' and see it off. This kind of behaviour helps to explain why, when young birds first return to Rutland Water, we only see them sporadically. When John Wright first identified 5R(04) at the reservoir in 2006, he was chased off by 03(97) and made only infrequent visits for the next few months. This is partly due to the wanderlust of young birds when they first return, but to a certain extent they're forced to behave in this way by the dominance of experienced, established adults. It's noticeable when analysing AW(06)'s satellite-tracking data from 2011 that he often avoided fishing at Rutland Water – probably because he is subordinate to the other, older birds.

It's not only at the fishing grounds that we observe interactions between Ospreys. At Site B, we ask the volunteers to record intrusions by other Ospreys. As the summer progresses and sub-adult birds become more frequent visitors to the reservoir, intrusions by these non-breeding birds become more regular at the established nests. This was

03(97), right, chasing 09(98) away from Site B, 2 May 2011. Intrusions like this sometimes force breeding males to invest more time in defending the nest, rather than fishing.

P6 missing

Ob(00)

P2 missing

32(05)

P7 half grown

big gap right of centre

nick in tip

gap left

gap right side of centre

new P1 half grown

P2 half grown

09(98)

P7 half grown

new P9 ½ grown

P8 missing

P7 ½ grown

Gaps

clean

nick in P3

gap

Lagoon 4 ♀

03(97)

5R(04)

P7 half grown

clean

new P9 ½ grown

6 Rutland Ospreys - 14/8/09
Site B

Because of numerous intrusions at Site B in 2009 03(97) had to spend more time than usual defending the nest. It was possible to identify five different intruding birds on this particular day, by comparing the differing stages of moult of each individual.

The Manton Bay female washing her feet close to the nest. After eating, Ospreys often fly low across the water trailing their feet to remove fish scales, sometimes drinking at the same time.

particularly apparent in the summer of 2009, when four non-breeding birds – 09(98), 5R(04), 32(05) and an unringed female – made repeated intrusions at Site B. 32(05) was an especially impertinent visitor to his natal site, repeatedly attempting to land on the nest. This kind of behaviour is driven by the fact that young Ospreys prefer to take over established territories rather than build their own nests from scratch. Long-established nests, like Site B, therefore become a focal point of activity. For the resident male, this has serious implications. Aside from providing fish for his family, he must defend his nest against intruders; leaving your mate to do this would invariably result in the eggs or chicks being left exposed for prolonged periods. Problems arise, therefore, when these intrusions become very regular. This is exactly what happened in summer 2009. It meant that 03(97) had to spend longer defending his nest, and therefore less time fishing. When he did go fishing he rarely went to the reservoir, preferring instead to visit the sites where he knew fish were

easier to come by. The problem with this was that fish from these other sites were smaller than the average reservoir trout or Roach, so there was less fish to divide amongst the family. Hierarchies develop among siblings in a nest and if there is insufficient food then the smallest, subordinate chick is usually the one to suffer. It seems no coincidence that 2009 is the only year when there has been a runt chick in the Site B nest. 03(97) simply wasn't able to dedicate enough time to fishing, because of the repeated intrusions by non-breeding birds. The problem was then compounded by the fact that the fish he was bringing back to the nest were not big enough for the family to share. Next summer, when there were fewer intrusions by non-breeding birds, 03(97) successfully raised three chicks once again.

By 2011 we were becoming used to the fact that Rainbow Trout was the most frequently caught species, but there were indications that the Roach population in Rutland Water was on the increase again. For the first time in several years

5R(04) fishing in Manton Bay.

fishermen started to report large shoals – not on the scale of a decade previously, but perhaps an indication that they were on the increase once again. A look at the data collected by the volunteers seemed to back this up. Both 03(97) and 5R(04) have begun to catch more Roach again. It will be interesting to see if this trend continues.

There are only two examples of Ospreys taking other prey at Rutland Water. In 2005 John Wright watched 05(00) pluck then partly eat a dead crow that she had picked up at Site B, mistaking it for nest lining. Then in March 2012, 5R(04) on one of his numerous fishing trips around Manton Bay caught a Red Signal crayfish. Unsurprisingly, he dropped this potentially painful meal before he had a chance to try and eat it. It would have been fascinating to see how he would have gone about it.

Adult Ospreys are supreme hunters, but the same cannot be said for juveniles. Manton Bay is one of the best places to watch fishing Ospreys at Rutland Water, particularly now the installation of a bund means we can control the water level throughout the summer. One of the best times to visit Shallow Water and Waderscrape Hides (which overlook the bay) is during late July and August, when the juvenile birds are making their first fishing attempts. Most young Ospreys don't catch a fish for themselves before they set out on migration, but the Manton Bay juveniles are at a distinct advantage compared with youngsters from other nests. Whereas, strangely, most Ospreys in the UK nest away from water, the Manton Bay nest is on a pole set in about 2 metres of water. This situation gives the young birds ample opportunity to practise fishing. And they certainly need the practice. More often than not their dives are clumsy half-hearted affairs and they are rarely successful. This emphasises what a steep learning curve the young birds have to overcome once they set out on their first migration to West Africa.

Whether it's watching the dramatic moment when an adult Osprey – a superbly well-adapted, fine-tuned predator – crashes into the water to pluck out a fine Rutland trout, or the altogether more comical attempts of a juvenile Osprey to catch its first fish, the success of the project means that watching fishing Ospreys at Rutland Water is a sight that is here to stay. And what a great thing that is too.

Fishing Ospreys often send up a big splash as they hit the water.

Volunteer Diary, Tom and Anne Price, 2010

Happiness is a spring morning, sitting quietly in a wildlife-rich habitat as the sun rises slowly into the sky. Such are the joys of an early shift as an Osprey volunteer, with the added bonus of watching a nesting pair of rare birds. However, in early April, on our first session of 2010, things were very different, with our senses being challenged as never before. The fog was as thick as we have seen it for years, perhaps only 10 metres visibility when the nest was over 30 metres away. It was impossible to witness any intrusion, but we were fortunate that it was still early in the season and the nesting pair was not yet incubating and was therefore less at risk from egg collectors.

Well, that's what we thought when we arrived at the hide, but we soon realised, after a little more thought, that Ospreys, like farmyard geese, are their own watchdogs. Ospreys have amazing eyesight so they would pick up on any intrusion into their personal nesting zone, and as we recalled previous shifts we could remember what their distress calls sounded like. So within minutes we'd figured this out and could relax a little, knowing that we could quickly walk to within sight of the nest if a problem arose. Our task, therefore, was to keep as quiet as possible and listen for any sound, as it was our only link with the Ospreys.

Fog normally discourages birds from both flying and singing, but it also has the almost counter-intuitive effect of making sound clearer, perhaps helped by the still air. For almost the entire shift there was virtually no bird song, but for long periods we were serenaded by the beautiful song of a single Mistle Thrush, probably perched on his favourite spot at the top of a tall tree just peeking into the sun above the blanket of fog. The Ospreys were also talking and we knew instinctively what 03 and his partner were saying: 'Erm 03.' 'Yes dear.' 'A fresh fish breakfast would be nice.' 'Well dear, as much as I want to, there is little point in trying to catch a fish that I cannot see.' This sort of conversation continued periodically and whilst 03 has a reputation for turning a deaf ear, today he had the perfect excuse.

Ken, our relief volunteer, strolled up out of the fog, and with little hope of it clearing soon we decided to head back home along the side of the wood. As we did so, Woodpigeons, which thought that we'd sneaked up on them, would make us jump as they launched themselves with great speed and noise from nearby hidden perches. Then as we crossed the fields we were clearly frightening groups of grazing rabbits, which ran panicking in all directions. By the time we got home, the sun had finally broken through revealing a cloudless blue sky. What a truly stunning morning it had been, an exclusive solo performance by a 'stormcock' and watching Ospreys by sound alone.

03 (97) Wing drying after heavy shower
Site B - 19·5·08.

An Incredible Journey: Migration

In early September, as the days become shorter and night-time temperatures begin to fall, juvenile Ospreys – many of which won't have been on the wing for much more than a month – prepare for the most hazardous period of their life, their first migration to Africa.

One of the recurring questions about the translocation project was the suggestion that, having been separated from their parents, the translocated birds would be at a disadvantage. Didn't they need to be taught how to fish? Surely they needed their parents to

Male 06(00) feeding his chicks in 2009. Females usually feed the youngsters, but sometimes their mate helps out too.

show them the way to Africa? This, however, is not the case. For young Ospreys, flying, fishing and migrating is all driven by instinct. Their first migration is unquestionably the most perilous period of their life, mainly because they must make the long and arduous flight alone. Not only this, but most juvenile birds won't have caught a fish for themselves before setting off on the 3,000-mile flight to the tropics.

Young Ospreys are usually completely dependent upon their father for food until the day they depart on migration.

Juvenile 03(08) departing on migration, 23 August 2008. She never returned to Rutland, choosing instead to breed on the Dyfi Estuary in Mid Wales.

Site B - 23.8.08

Very sunny and warm am and early pm with a light SW breeze, an ideal day for migration.
When I arrived at 08.30 the juvenile ♀ (03) was food-begging on the nest and the adult ♂ was in the near ash tree. He eventually gave in to the food begging and departed se. ♀ (03) then began circling over the spinney, joining her brother (05) for a bit of play-chasing in the warm blue sky. A few minutes later she landed in the ash tree and was sat preening and staring intently south. Just after 10am she took off and flew straight towards me, circling 100ft above my head before quickly gaining height. I had to

really concentrate on her as she became smaller and smaller in the cloudless sky. Then, suddenly, she glided south at a height of maybe 1500-2000ft and was lost to view - her migration had started!
She had gone from food begging on the nest, to play fighting with her brother and finally migrating south all in the space of 30 minutes.
My thoughts will now be with her for the rest of the day, wondering just how far she will get today and ultimately when will she catch her first fish.
Migration is quite simply amazing.

Juvenile setting off on migration - August

Anyone who has visited an Osprey nest in late summer will be able to vouch for this – the incessant and monotonous food-begging calls of recently fledged juveniles demonstrate that they're not yet ready for independence. Male Ospreys, therefore, have a vital role to play in the weeks leading up to the departure of their offspring. They must fill them with as much fish as possible to ensure the young birds are in the best possible condition when they depart. It will take them many attempts to hone their fishing technique and if they're not in

good condition when they set out on migration the chances are that they won't survive for more than a few weeks as they head south. This of course was one of the great advantages of the translocation – we could ensure that the translocated birds had as much fresh fish as they wanted before they left. Just as adult males do, we continued to provide fish for the youngsters until they embarked on their first migration. We hoped this would give them that all-important helping hand as they made the quick switch to independence.

TRACKING THE BIRDS SOUTH

One of the most important elements of a young Osprey's first migration from the UK is the direction it departs in. That seems an obvious point to make, but due to the UK's position on the edge of Western Europe if the young birds head too far south-west when they set off, they immediately get into trouble. The big problem is that migration is inherent. Research suggests that Swedish Ospreys may have been important in the recolonisation of Scotland. Swedish birds also winter in West Africa, so are predisposed to fly south-west. The instinctive nature of a young Osprey's first migration, therefore, results in a very strong urge to head west of south. This is not necessarily a problem, but if the birds go too far south-west they can find themselves out in the Bay of Biscay. We know this thanks to satellite tracking. Over the course of the past decade our understanding of migration has been greatly enhanced by advances in satellite-tracking technology. Ringing had enabled us to identify key wintering areas for Ospreys and other migratory birds, but satellite tracking has provided answers to many more questions about the epic flights of Ospreys and many other species.

In 1999 satellite tracking was still in its infancy. A few storks, eagles and Ospreys had been tracked elsewhere in Europe, but it was certainly cutting-edge science. Two North American companies had developed trackers that weighed between 30 and 40g – light enough to be fitted to an Osprey without causing the bird undue problems – and excitingly, thanks to funding from Anglian Water, we were able to tag a number of birds from Rutland and Scotland. We knew from ringing recoveries that the majority of our birds would head towards the West African coast – from southern Mauritania, south towards Guinea, but how long would it take them to get there, and what route would they take? Satellite tracking, we hoped, would provide the answers. It would also shed more light on why mortality was very high among young Ospreys – as few as 30% survive the first two years of their life – but what was it about the first migration that was particularly hazardous? The tracking would also enable us to compare the routes of translocated birds with adults and juveniles from Scotland. It was exciting to think how much we would be able to learn.

Although Ospreys are ringed when they're six weeks old, we felt it was important to wait longer before fitting the satellite transmitters. The great advantage of having the translocated birds in the release pens was that we were able to wait until the day before release before fitting the transmitters – not a straightforward task – which sit on the bird's back like a small backpack, and are secured in place with four pieces of Teflon that are then sewn together with cotton. It's important to get it exactly right: too loose and the transmitter will move about on the bird's back; too tight and it may cause lacerations and discomfort. In those early years the transmitters had a very limited lifespan, perhaps no more than a year for the battery-powered devices. We felt it was important that the birds were free of the transmitters once they'd stopped collecting data and, by fixing the harness in place with cotton, we hoped that eventually the

Roy Dennis, Tim Appleton and Helen McIntyre fitting a satellite transmitter to a translocated juvenile before release.

Juvenile migrating across the sea. Ospreys travel at varying altitudes during their migration and, unlike some raptors, can make long sea crossings.

thread would rot and the transmitter would fall off. Fitting the transmitters took no more than 15 minutes and the birds were then put back in the pens ahead of their release the next day. Once the birds had preened, the transmitters were fairly inconspicuous, and it's often only the 15cm aerial that is visible in the field. In all, we equipped 14 of the translocated juveniles with transmitters and Roy tagged another 13 Scottish birds. In the third year we used solar-powered transmitters for the first time: these, it was hoped, would have a much longer lifespan.

Having equipped the birds with transmitters and checked that the data-collection process was working – this was done through the Argos tracking system based in France – it was a case of waiting for the birds to leave. It was hugely exciting but also extremely nerve-racking. We knew that many hazards lay in wait for the birds and now we were going to see exactly why that first migration was such an arduous time for the young birds. By late August the birds began to leave and a pattern was immediately apparent. Of the 14 birds we tracked from Rutland Water, 13 began their migration west of south. For some this wasn't a problem; they headed into Sussex and Hampshire, then across the English Channel to Normandy. For others, though, it was a different story. A good example was bird 09(00), in 2000, who left Rutland Water on 2 September and headed south through the Chilterns that afternoon. Next morning we received a series of signals off the Brittany coast suggesting that 09(00) had

crossed the Channel during the night. Having just missed landfall in France, 09(00) continued on the same south-westerly course across the Bay of Biscay. Fourteen hours later the next batch of signals suggested that, sadly, she had just failed to reach the northern coast of Spain. For the next two weeks we received a series of signals consistent with the bird's body floating in the sea. Birdwatchers in northern Spain have sometimes reported exhausted migrant Ospreys coming in off the Bay of Biscay and being mobbed by Yellow-legged Gulls. Under normal circumstances an Osprey would have little difficulty in evading these attacks, but for 09(00), who had covered more than 750 miles non-stop since leaving the Hampshire coast, it was perhaps just too much, forcing her down into the sea.

09(00) was not the only victim of the Bay of Biscay. Next year we received a series of signals from 04(01)'s transmitter, suggesting that she too had drowned off the Spanish coast; the readings from her transmitter appeared to show her floating in the sea, just as 09(00) had done the previous year. Then, a few weeks later we received news that on 12 September 04(01)'s body had been found in the water off a beach near Tuineje, Fuerteventura. This was over 1,000 miles from the last position the bird's transmitter had recorded and showed that, having flown south-west across the Bay of Biscay, 04(01) appeared to have missed the Spanish coast and continued on that same course towards the Canary Islands. Sadly, she had then just failed to make land.

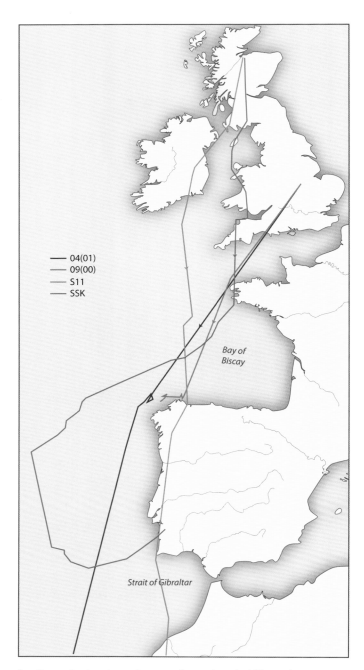

Satellite tracking has shown that many Ospreys from the UK begin their migration in a south-westerly direction, taking them out across the Bay of Biscay. Sadly some do not survive: 09(00) drowned off the coast of northern Spain and 04(01) washed up dead on the Canary Islands after missing the Spanish coast altogether. Others, however, do make it. SSK completed a 64-hour non-stop flight after being blown out into the Atlantic by a storm, and S11 landed on a boat halfway across the Bay of Biscay, providing her with a much-needed break.

It soon became clear that for young Ospreys from the UK, the Bay of Biscay was a very real hazard. Our early tracking showed that while Ospreys are extremely powerful fliers – and can make long sea crossings – for inexperienced juveniles who have been on the wing for little more than a month, these extended periods in the air are incredibly demanding.

Sometimes the birds need luck on their side if they're going to survive. That is exactly what happened to S11, one of the Scottish birds we were tracking in 2000. Having migrated south-west from her nest in the north-east Highlands, S11 found herself at the southern tip of Ireland. None the wiser as to the vast area of open ocean that lay ahead, S11 headed out across the sea. Twelve hours later she was only halfway across and now flying in complete darkness. There seemed every chance that she would drop, exhausted, into the sea. Fortunately a passing cargo ship came to her rescue. When we reviewed S11's progress across the Bay of Biscay it was noticeable that halfway across she had slowed right down. The only possible explanation is that she landed on a ship and was able to rest up for a few hours. This almost certainly saved her, giving her a vital break from the long crossing. When she resumed her flight south she had enough energy to reach the coast of northern Spain. She had covered an incredible 625 miles across the open ocean over the course of 36 hours – a remarkable flight for a bird with so little experience.

It was incredibly exciting to be charting these epic flights for the first time. We knew that the birds made these journeys every year, but to be able to follow the progress of individuals we knew so well really brought the migration to life. It was also providing us with completely new information. For the first time we could say for certain that Ospreys will migrate at night if they have to.

Undoubtedly the most incredible of all the night-time flights we recorded was in 2002. That year Roy fitted one of his remaining transmitters to a juvenile female. Like several of the other birds we had followed, she migrated south through western parts of the UK, then headed out over the English Channel towards Brittany. Rather than resting in France she then continued south-west across the Bay of Biscay. Her initial flight path was good, but then she hit problems. Although several of the adult birds we've followed have undertaken long sea crossings, they only ever made such flights when the weather was favourable. SSK, in contrast, was heading out into a storm. A low pressure over Portugal was creating strong easterly winds across the Bay of Biscay and as SSK flew south she was pushed further and further west – 36 hours later she was out in the middle of the Atlantic and still being blown south-west into the vast open ocean. She appeared doomed. Fortunately the weather system that had caused her to be blown off course then came to her rescue. Over the course of the next few hours she was blown south and then east around the low pressure. Eventually, 64 hours after leaving the English coast, she made landfall in Portugal having covered a remarkable 1,500 miles over the sea. Having finally made land she then remained in Portugal for the rest of the winter. Three years later she raised chicks of her own at a nest in southern Scotland. Although her transmitter was no longer working, we felt sure that she would have learnt from

Fishing Osprey upsetting roosting Black-tailed Godwits – l'Aiguillon-Sur-Mer – 7.9.09

her mistakes on that first flight south and kept to the French coast as she flew south in future years.

Over the past decade further advances in satellite tracking have enhanced our knowledge of Osprey migration even more. It's especially interesting to compare the flights of adults and juveniles. While the juveniles we were following were undertaking their first migration to West Africa, many of the adult birds we've tracked have completed numerous flights south and know the journey well. In 2011 we fitted two adult male birds at Rutland Water with new GPS transmitters. The new transmitters weigh the same as the old-style transmitters we'd used ten years previously, but are considerably more sophisticated. A transmitter records a bird's location every hour, data that are accurate to within 15 metres. It also logs the bird's speed, altitude and orientation, providing us with unprecedented detail. Whereas most of the juvenile birds we had tracked had set out in a south-westerly direction, it was revealing that the two adult birds we tracked in 2011 – 09(98) and AW(06) – both set off on a distinctly south-easterly course. In fact their route from Rutland Water to the Kent coast was almost identical. Both birds headed south-east into Essex and across the eastern outskirts of London. They then set out across the English Channel from Dungeness. By crossing the Channel here, both birds arrived safely in France then continued south past Paris and onwards towards Orleans Forest, where 30 pairs of Ospreys breed each year.

Migration at First hand

Although 09(98) and AW(06) both flew through the centre of France, many adult Ospreys follow the Atlantic coast as they head south. In 2009 John Wright and I decided to follow the same route south through France. We set off in John's car from Rutland Water at 9pm on 6 September and by early next morning we were driving south through France. In early September the French coast is alive with bird migration. Migrant passerines – Wrynecks, Bluethroats and warblers – skulk in coastal vegetation, and flocks of passage waders interrupt their flight south to feed up in the rich estuaries. We arrived at L'Aguillon just north of La Rochelle shortly after midday on 7 September and scanned the estuary. A large flock of Black-tailed Godwits was busy feeding in front of us; birds probably heading for Spain for the winter. Beyond them we located our first Osprey, perched on a distant post in the middle of the estuary. It was exciting to think that this could be a bird from Rutland Water. The bird was too distant and the heat haze too bad to see if it was ringed, but we knew that many of our Rutland birds would pass through this area each autumn. We could at least tell that the bird was an adult female. The chances were that this bird probably stopped off at the estuary every year. Satellite-tracking studies have

Osprey at L'Aguillon-sur-Mer, September 2010. The Atlantic coast of France is an excellent place to see migrating Ospreys in the autumn.

Osprey with Bar-tailed Godwits, Ile d'Oleron, September 2011.

Osprey fishing at Ile d'Oleron, September 2011.

shown that although the adult birds take slightly different routes each year – varying with wind and other climatic factors – they will usually head to known stopover points somewhere in Europe. Their favoured site is often somewhere they lingered during their first flight south and a place where they know they can feed and rest up before resuming their journey. Some birds will linger at these sites for no more than a day, whereas others stay for a week or more. As we looked out across the estuary we wondered how long this particular female would stay. As we watched she took off and began circling the estuary, flushing a huge flock of Knot as she did. The whirling mass of waders and fishing Osprey made for a truly evocative sight.

Just south of L'Aguillon is Ile d'Oleron, an island 19 miles long and 7 miles wide. It is another great place to watch migration and is where Nimrod, an adult male Osprey satellite tagged by Roy Dennis, stops off each autumn. Separated from the French mainland by a wide estuary, the abundant fish stocks provide a rich hunting ground for migrant Ospreys. When John Wright and I visited in early September 2010, Nimrod was still in Scotland but an unringed male was stopping off in a bay on the east side of the island. We spent a morning watching him fishing just offshore as migrant Willow Warblers and a single Wryneck searched for food in the coastal scrub nearby; another reminder that the protection of stopover sites is important for more than just Ospreys. Over the course of 48 hours on Ile d'Oleron we must have seen at least 15 individual Ospreys, some heading purposefully south, but most taking advantage of the opportunity to feed and rest up.

Migrant Ospreys fly south through Europe, and our studies have shown that there is often a clear distinction between the routes used by adults and juveniles. Most of the adult birds we've followed avoid long crossings of the Bay of Biscay by flying south through France. If they've made a mistake during a previous migration – like SSK did in 2002 – they appear to learn from it. It seems that the birds are able to refine their migration over successive journeys. Mirja, a Finnish Osprey tracked by Professor Pertti Saurola of the University of Helsinki, is perhaps the best example of this. In 2002 Mirja was fitted with a solar-powered transmitter before her first autumn migration. The transmitter showed that she flew south through Eastern Europe and Greece and then into Libya. From there she flew in a wide arc across the eastern Sahara to Cameroon. It was not the most direct of flights but she had reached a wintering area favoured by many Finnish Ospreys. Her transmitter continued to provide data for another three and a half years and her migration route became more direct over successive journeys. It seemed that she was learning from her mistakes and perhaps using recognisable geographical features to guide her on her way (for more information on Osprey Mirja, see http://www.luomus.fi/english/zoology/satelliteospreys/index.htm).

THE MOUNTAINS AWAIT

Like Mirja, it was clear that 09(98) and AW(06) had refined their own migrations over successive journeys and both were now expert navigators. As he flew south through France AW(06) switched to a more south-westerly course, thereby avoiding the Pyrenees. 09(98), on the other hand, flew straight through the mountains. This proved what John and I had suspected as we drove south through France in autumn 2009 – that while some adult birds from Rutland Water avoid the Pyrenees by heading south along the Atlantic coast, others fly through the mountains. With this in mind we headed for Organbidexka, a spectacular migration watchpoint in the western Pyrenees. As we drove through the small village of Trois-Villes, approaching the mountains from the north, John suddenly slammed on the brakes – he'd seen a bird of prey circling over the village. Myself and Paul Waterhouse, a friend and ex-colleague who was travelling with us, clambered out to have a look. It was a juvenile Osprey. With the foreboding mountains in the distance the Osprey appeared unsure of what to do next. It circled the

Juvenile ♂ Osprey fishing – ILE D'OLERON – 2·9·10

village, then slowly drifted towards the mountains. It was too late in the day to pass over the high peaks now, so the bird would have to find somewhere to roost for the night. This chance encounter really helped to emphasise what a demanding time this was for juvenile Ospreys heading south for the first time. Each day they had to make decisions that would have a major bearing on whether they would survive their first migration or not.

As we arrived at Organbidexka the next morning we were greeted by a spectacular sunrise over the jagged peaks that surround the viewpoint. We were now almost 2,000 metres up in the mountains and, as mist hung in the valleys below, the first birds began moving. First a Marsh Harrier then a group of four Honey-buzzards circled to gain height, then drifted leisurely past. Honey-buzzards pass through Organbidexka in their thousands in late August and although we were now past that peak period, we expected to see these mysterious raptors in reasonable numbers. Honey-buzzards, like many other migrant birds of prey, often migrate in large flocks – it's not unusual to see groups of more than 50 individuals at Organbidexka – and in many ways this gives young Honey-buzzards a big advantage over migrating Ospreys. The young buzzards simply follow the adults to sub-Saharan Africa, but young Ospreys must navigate themselves. Sure enough, the first Osprey we picked up at 8am was heading purposefully through the mountains alone.

We stayed at the watchpoint all day, enthralled by the sight of passing groups of Honey-buzzards, Black Storks and Black Kites. Every so often another Osprey would power through the mountain passes. Once the watchers from Mision Migration, the French organisation that runs the counts, realised who we were, every passing Osprey was greeted by a great deal of excitement and cheering; I doubt whether Ospreys had ever received quite so much attention at Organbidexka before. In all 25 Ospreys passed over the watchpoint that day.

Our satellite-tracking studies have shown that adult birds generally make quite leisurely progress through Europe, stopping each evening to fish and rest after a day's flight of around 200 miles. Once clear of the Pyrenees a series of fairly large reservoirs on the southern edge of the mountains provides a good place to do just that. After a couple of days at Organbidexka, John, Paul and I continued south through the mountains, stopping off at Embalse de Yesa. We scanned the shoreline and, sure enough, there was an adult Osprey perched on a tree stump just back from the water's edge. We wondered if it was one of the birds we'd seen flying through the mountains the previous day. Next autumn, when we repeated the journey, we saw an Osprey on exactly the same perch. The birds are such creatures of habit that there was every chance this was the same bird as the one seen the previous September.

Migrating Osprey at Col d'Organbidexka, September 2010.

Col d'Organbidexka, a migration watchpoint situated in the western Pyrenees. On a good day up to 25 Ospreys can be seen migrating through the mountain pass.

Juvenile ♂ Osprey passing through the Pyrenees – September

Osprey – Embalse de Yesa – 8.9.10. Almost in the same dead tree as last year!

Migrant Ospreys sometimes stop off at the same places each year. We saw an Osprey perched on the same dead tree at Embalse de Yesa in north-east Spain in two consecutive autumns and it may well have been the same individual.

The wind turbines near Tarifa present an obvious hazard to migrating birds, especially in poor visibility.

White Storks

Egyptian Vulture and Short-toed Eagle

Short-toed Eagle

Honey-buzzard

Booted Eagle

Thousands of raptors and storks converge in southern Spain each autumn before making the short flight across the Strait of Gibraltar to Africa.

For those juvenile Ospreys who survive crossing the Bay of Biscay, the northern coast of Spain provides a much-needed chance to rest up before they continue further south. Estuaries such as Urdaibai near Bilbao provide rich hunting grounds – just the place to refine your fishing technique. From there the birds continue south on a broad front towards southern Spain and Portugal. Searing temperatures in the heart of Spain provide thermals that make the journey much easier. As he flew across the arid plains, AW(06) reached altitudes of more than 2,700 metres.

We had assumed that most of our satellite-tagged birds would power on through Spain and into Morocco, but some surprised us by wintering in Spain and Portugal. 06(01), the young female who returned to breed at Rutland Water in 2003, was a good example. Having reached Portugal she spent the winter on Rio Tajo. S06, one of the adult birds tagged by Roy Dennis, wintered even further north, at Embalse de Gabriel y Galan, a large reservoir in Extremadura in central Spain. Roy was even able to travel down to Spain to see her. This seems to reflect an increasing trend among northern European Ospreys to winter in Iberia, which actually makes perfect sense. By only flying as far south as Spain and Portugal the migration is much shorter and, unlike the birds who continue on to West Africa, they don't need to negotiate the Sahara. There seems every chance that more and more Ospreys from the UK will choose to spend the winter in Iberia; the theory of natural selection suggesting that this trait will be passed through to future generations.

Osprey, Black kites and a short-toed Eagle over Tarifa – September.

Africa in Sight

Having said this, most Ospreys from the UK do continue into Africa. As the various flights across the Bay of Biscay have demonstrated, Ospreys are able to make long sea crossings and so, unlike many other migrant birds of prey, they cross the Mediterranean on a broad front. Some fly from the western coast of Spain and Portugal direct to Morocco, while others head across the Mediterranean close to Marbella. AW(06) did this in 2011, flying 75 miles across the sea at an altitude of between 10 and 20 metres. 09(98), in contrast, made a definite change of direction to enable him to make the short hop across the Strait of Gibraltar. Here just 10 miles of sea separate Europe and Africa and for most migrant birds of prey – most of whom are far more dependent on thermals than Ospreys – this is the only place they can cross. As 09(98) headed across the sea at Tarifa, with the mountains of northern Morocco prominent on the horizon, he would have been joined by thousands of Short-toed Eagles, Black Kites, Booted Eagles and Honey-buzzards. In 2009 and 2010, John, Paul and I concluded our migration trip at the Migres migration watchpoints close to Tarifa. On a good day with the right weather conditions this is a truly spectacular place to watch migration. It's awe-inspiring to see thousands of birds of prey heading out across the sea towards Morocco.

Like the Atlantic coast of France and the estuaries of northern Spain, the coast of southern Spain is a good place for Ospreys to rest during their migration. In autumn 2010 John Wright saw the same Scottish-ringed juvenile, blue/white UB, each time he visited Palmones Marsh, just west of Gibraltar. At the time John wondered if the young male would winter in Spain, but it later transpired that, in fact, he continued further south. Just over a year later UB was photographed at the Sine-Saloum Delta in Senegal. Similarly, in 2000, one of the satellite-tagged translocated birds, 03(00), spent three months stopping over near Cadiz, before resuming his migration to West Africa in December.

Once in Morocco the experienced adult birds head south-west, taking them past Fes and Marrakech and on towards the Atlas Mountains. These mountains, rising to more than 3,500 metres in places, provide a very obvious barrier to migrating birds of prey. The adult birds know this and both 09(98) and AW(06) flew west along the north side of the mountains before turning south towards Agadir. By doing so they had intentionally avoided the high peaks that lie further to the east. Some juveniles followed this same route, but others didn't. Perhaps the best example was bird 01(00). He made swift progress through Europe and crossed the Mediterranean to the Morocco–Algeria border on 9 September 2000. Rather than heading south-west 01(00) simply continued on the southerly course he had maintained through Spain. Unknowingly this

Juvenile male Osprey fishing on the beach at Tarifa. An increasing number of birds are choosing to winter in southern Spain and Portugal.

route would result in him having to make an even more arduous crossing of the desert.

Having reached the northern edge of the Sahara, all of the adult birds we've tracked have followed roughly the same south-westerly course across one of the most inhospitable parts of the planet. 09(98) and AW(06) maintained a remarkably similar route as they flew south-west through Morocco, Western Sahara and Mauritania. Whereas 09(98), in particular, had flown through Europe at a fairly leisurely pace, now was not a time to hang around. All the adult birds we've tracked have flown further each day across the Sahara than they did in northern Europe; and with good reason. Unlike further north, the birds now had to migrate for several days without food. As a result, they just wanted to cross the desert as quickly as possible. It was no surprise, therefore, that we recorded maximum speeds for both 09(98) and AW(06) in the Sahara, with 09(98) topping 50mph on at least one occasion.

Our tracking had shown that the birds sometimes migrate at night, especially during long sea crossings, but the new GPS transmitters indicate that, generally, they do not do so over the desert. On his first day in the northern Sahara, AW(06) continued migrating until around 2am, but that was the only occasion that either he or 09(98) migrated in darkness across the desert. Every other evening they would end their day's flight at around 6 or 7pm, roosting on the desert floor. The satellite-tracking data suggest that the birds use distinctive geographical landmarks to help them

Juvenile Osprey roosting on the desert floor.

navigate and several of the birds we've tracked appear to have followed the same ridge system south-west across the northern edge of the Sahara. Perhaps this explains why they usually choose not to fly at night across the Sahara?

By crossing the western part of the Sahara it generally takes the adult birds three to four days to cross the desert, but for the juveniles who used a more easterly route, the flight was longer. It took 01(00) six days to fly south through Algeria and Mali, so the young male must have been exhausted by the time he reached a tributary of the River Niger in the southern part of Mali. Sadly not all of the juveniles we've tracked have survived crossing the desert. The seven birds who used the same westerly route as the adults all made it across, but

Ospreys wintering at Tanji, Gambia Jan 2011

four birds died further to the east in Algeria and Mali. The decision to fly south-west rather than south, therefore, was often a question of life or death.

Having crossed the desert the adult birds fly to their regular wintering site. If they haven't broken up their journey with a stopover, the entire migration may have taken little more than two weeks. Our satellite-tracking work has shown that adults return to the same site each winter, perching on the same trees and fishing in the same places each day. For Ospreys from the UK this wintering site can be anywhere along the West African coast, from Mauritania south to Guinea and perhaps even Sierra Leone, Liberia or the Ivory Coast. Some winter inland, but the majority of birds favour the coast where vast river deltas and shallow seas provide rich hunting grounds.

An adult male chasing a juvenile male at the River Allahein on the border of The Gambia and Senegal, January 2011. Aggression from adults results in juveniles wandering widely when they first arrive in West Africa.

A WINTER HOME

In January 2011 and 2012 myself and a team of staff and volunteers from the project travelled to West Africa to learn more about the birds' lives on the wintering grounds. Satellite tracking provides us with a unique way of following the birds during the winter, but there is nothing quite like seeing them for real.

One of the most interesting findings of our satellite-tracking research has been demonstrating how widely young birds range during their first winter in Africa. Having successfully negotiated the Sahara the juveniles must find somewhere to spend the winter. On the face of it this seems a relatively simple task. There is a plethora of suitable habitat along the coast of West Africa, but the most significant challenge for the young birds is not finding somewhere where

food is plentiful – it's more about choosing a location where they are accepted by the established wintering adults. Our satellite-tagged juveniles often wander widely during their first few months in West Africa and this is often due to hierarchies that exist at many of the most favourable wintering sites.

On numerous occasions during our trip in 2011 we witnessed juvenile birds being chased by adults; it was clear that many of these established birds were behaving very territorially. They appeared to accept the presence of other adult birds – many of which they would have known from previous winters – but if a juvenile ventured too close, there was trouble. The adult would give chase, forcing the youngster

Juvenile female Osprey on Bijoli Island, The Gambia, January 2011.

to search for somewhere else to fish. For some unlucky juvenile birds this must happen again and again. Wherever they go, they're hassled by established adults. It is for this reason that young birds range so widely when they first arrive in Africa. The hierarchies that exist at the best fishing grounds can have serious implications for juvenile birds. Ringing recoveries had shown that as few as 30% of young Ospreys survive the first two years of their lives. You might reasonably assume that this is due to the hazards of the first migration – and our initial satellite tracking showed that the first migration did take its toll – but this alone did not explain this very high mortality. So what other factors were to blame?

In West Africa heavy rains fall from July to September. During this period many of the seasonal water bodies are replenished after completely drying out during the winter. For the newly arrived juvenile Ospreys this is very important. Because they're frequently forced away from the prime sites on the coast, juveniles often depend on this marginal habitat. After such a long and arduous journey, many of the young birds arrive in West Africa in relatively poor condition. They may not yet have perfected their fishing technique – during our trip we regularly saw juveniles struggling to catch fish at sites where adult birds were having very little difficulty – so it's essential they find a site where fishing is relatively simple. A wet rainy season ensures that there are plenty of these sites – and therefore food – to sustain them, but in drier years, things are more difficult. Perhaps that was the problem for 01(00)? Having reached the tributary of the River Niger in southern Mali, 01(00) was still a long way from the West African coast. Instinctively he knew this and the day after arriving at the first water he had seen for almost a week, he resumed his migration, flying south-west towards Liberia. Two days later he changed direction again, this time heading north into Mauritania. Then, upon reaching the southern edge of the Sahara, he changed course for a third time, heading due west towards the coast. When he finally reached a lake in the north of Senegal he had covered a remarkable 4,660 miles in just over a month. Like many of the juveniles we'd tracked, 01(00) had not ended up in a favourable area. The lake he had chosen was probably a seasonal one and perhaps it didn't hold the same abundant supply of fish as the better sites on the coast? Whatever the case, 01(00) must have been exhausted after his long migration and, sadly, he died a month after reaching northern Senegal. If he had been able to settle at a site where fishing was easier, he may have survived.

An added danger for young birds at some of these poorer quality sites is predation by feral dogs and jackals, which in dry years can wade out into the shallow water. Should a young Osprey get into difficulty when fishing – as they often do – it would make fairly easy pickings. So in short, getting across the Sahara and arriving in West Africa is no guarantee a young Osprey will survive.

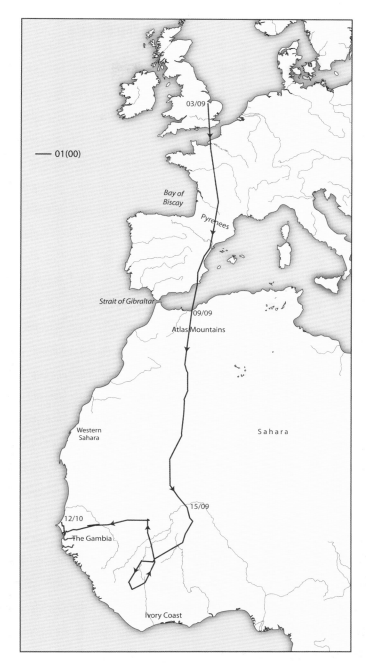

01(00)'s migration from Rutland to northern Senegal in autumn 2000.

For adult birds, on the other hand, the winter is a very easy time. In Rutland 09(98) regularly travels 10 or 15 miles in search of food, but on the West African coast things are very different. Like the adult birds tracked by Roy Dennis, 09(98) has a very small 'home' range in winter – a short section of Senegalese coast south of St Louis. At this site fishing must be very easy, and the satellite data suggest that 09(98) generally only needs to make short forays out to sea once or twice a day. The rest of his day is spent on a favoured perch, one he uses every winter. Like 09(98), AW(06) initially headed to the West African coast. After a very fast migration he arrived on the coast of Guinea less than two weeks after leaving

Adult female Osprey, Lampsar River, Senegal, February 2011.

The rivers of northern Senegal provide a wealth of suitable overwintering habitat. On a trip there in January 2011 members of the project team encountered numerous Ospreys fishing at low tide, when shallow water makes fish easier to catch.

Adult male Osprey, Senegal River, January 2011.

Osprey carrying a fish the wrong way round, The Gambia.

Osprey with a Needlefish, The Gambia. Needlefish are often caught by Ospreys on their West African wintering grounds.

Ospreys at Ile d'Oiseaux, Senegal, January 2011. At the best fishing sites the birds can be surprisingly tolerant of each other and less territorial than elsewhere. On this island in the Sine-Saloum Delta 14 birds – the majority of which were adults – could be seen perched within 200 metres of each other.

Rutland Water, having covered an average of more than 230 miles each day. He remained on the same short section of coastline for the next three months and we presumed this was his established wintering site. Like 09(98) he made short fishing trips out to sea each day but spent most of his time on favoured perches just back from the shore. Then suddenly, and without any warning, he left. On 17 December 2011, AW(06) headed south along the Guinea coast, passing the capital Conakry and continuing on towards Sierra Leone. He continued migrating for the next three days, passing through Sierra Leone and Liberia before finally settling in central-eastern Ivory Coast, some 1,000km from his original spot on the Guinean coast. It was a quite remarkable movement and one that suggested his time on the Guinea coast was nothing more than an extended stopover; his true winter home was in fact a short section of the River Lobo in the Ivory Coast.

It is fact that adult birds are faithful to the same wintering sites each year, which means that hierarchies exists at most sites along the West African coast. Along rivers such as the Allahein – which forms the southern border between The Gambia and Senegal – Ospreys can be found perched every few hundred metres along the mangroves and, as a result, juveniles must work hard to be accepted by the established adults. Likewise at Tanji in The Gambia, we found that six or seven adult Ospreys often perch together in an area of marsh just inland from the coast. They accept the presence of one another, but rarely allow juveniles to perch with them.

The one location that we visited where adult birds appeared more tolerant of juveniles was the Sine-Saloum

Scottish-ringed Osprey with Slender-billed Gulls, Sine-Saloum Delta, January 2011.

Osprey at Sine-Saloum Delta, Senegal, January 2011.

Adult female Osprey with Grey-headed Gull, Tanji, January 2011.

Delta in Senegal. This vast area of mangroves, estuary and shallow sea is one of the most important wintering sites for Ospreys in Africa. On a boat ride out to Ile d'Oiseaux during our 2011 trip we got a sense of what a very special place it really is. Leaving the village of Missirah at dawn we slowly chugged our way through the mangroves. As the sun appeared over the horizon, we saw our first Osprey – a German-ringed male perched in the mangroves. Moments later a second bird began hovering in front of the boat, looking for its first meal of the day. Missirah is around 8 miles from the mouth of the delta and as we got closer to the sea we encountered more and more Ospreys; some perched on sandbars, others fishing. After an hour and a half we reached our destination, the small sandy island of Ile d'Oiseaux. Little Bee-eaters darted through the sparse vegetation and Slender-billed Gulls flew back and forth overhead. At the western end of the island a sandy bar juts out into the sea. Scanning along the sandbar we counted 14 Ospreys perched within 200 metres of each other, including four birds sitting on the same piece of dead wood. That summer we had ten breeding Ospreys in Rutland – here were 14 birds perched together. It was an incredible sight. Several individuals had colour rings, including birds from Germany and Scotland, but perhaps the most notable thing was a complete lack of aggression. At every other site we'd visited we had watched adults chasing juveniles, but here there was none of that. Perhaps there was so much food that there was simply no need for the adult birds to waste energy chasing juveniles? The birds that were fishing around the boat certainly took very little time to catch fish. Having made a successful dive they would return to the sandbar and eat their fish on the ground, watched by Turnstones, Sanderlings and Slender-billed Gulls. One plucky Slender-billed Gull we watched even managed to take a few pieces of an Osprey's fish. It was a truly unforgettable morning and demonstrated what an important place the Sine-Saloum is for European Ospreys.

Osprey foot at Tanji, The Gambia. On the wintering grounds the birds face hazards, including discarded fishing nets and intentional killing.

Adult Osprey fishing at Tanji.

THREATS REMAIN

Visiting sites such as the Sine-Saloum it's easy to understand why Ospreys can live for so long (it is not uncommon for them to live into their twenties). Once adult birds have found a suitable wintering site and perfected their migration, they face few dangers. They expend very little energy on the wintering grounds and this helps to ensure that they're in good condition for the spring migration. The only real hazards they face during the winter are caused by humans. Many of the coastal communities depend on the sea for a living and discarded fishing nets present an obvious danger for adult and juvenile birds alike. Furthermore, in some

areas, Ospreys and other birds are killed indiscriminately, often by children. For this reason education is hugely important. We believe that the education programme we're running in West Africa and the project to link schools along Osprey migration flyways described later in this book are fundamental to the future conservation of migratory birds in West Africa and further afield.

Sadly, the need for this education was demonstrated early in 2012. Following his move to the Ivory Coast a couple of months earlier, AW(06) had remained faithful to a short 1.5-mile stretch of the River Lobo in the central part of the country. Then, in early February, he began to spend an increasing amount of time 20 miles away on the northernmost reaches of the vast Lac de Buyo. He spent most

French-ringed adult male Osprey on the Gambia–Senegal border, January 2012. Adult birds return to the same site each winter and we saw this bird, ringed by Rolf Wahl, during trips to the River Allahein in 2011 and 2012.

days at the lake, then returned to the river each evening to roost. There was nothing in his behaviour to suggest that anything was wrong, but we suddenly stopped receiving data from his transmitter on 18 February 2012. The last GPS transmissions we received were on 17 February. The last three positions, for 6am, 7am and 8am that morning, all give exactly the same location and the only data we received subsequently were six non-GPS positions 24 hours later on 18 February, which suggested that AW(06) was still in the same spot. This was confirmed by the transmitter's activity meter, which also showed he was not moving.

Although the satellite imagery for this part of the Ivory Coast is very poor the last positions we received are from what appear to be an area of cleared ground – not the sort of spot you would expect Ospreys to roost in, and certainly not somewhere they're likely to linger for 24 hours. The satellite data show that on the evening of 16 February AW(06) had been perched – perhaps on a dead tree in shallow water – a few hundred metres out from the shore. It's likely that many of the locals living around the lake are fishermen, so perhaps he became tangled in a discarded net and drowned, but there's also a chance that he was intentionally killed. In *Living on the Edge: Wetlands and Birds in a Changing Sahel*, a fantastic book that highlights the conservation issues facing birds in sub-Saharan Africa, Zwarts et al. (2009) suggest that persecution is often more of a problem inland than on the coast. In inland areas people tend to be concentrated around lakes and birds inhabiting these sites are, therefore, more likely to be intentionally taken. This emphasises why our education work in West Africa is so important. During our trip in 2012 many people expressed the view that if the local communities had a greater understanding of the journeys undertaken by Ospreys and other migratory birds, they would be far more willing to protect them.

IDENTIFYING INDIVIDUALS

Aside from adding to our understanding of the wintering ecology of Ospreys, our trips to West Africa gave us the opportunity to look for colour-ringed birds. We hoped we would find a Rutland bird, but in reality that was unlikely. We now knew that the birds winter over a vast area, so the chances of finding one from Rutland were extremely slim. That said, we came extremely close to finding one in 2011. By the middle of our fourth week in Gambia and Senegal we'd identified Ospreys from at least four different countries. German birds were by far the most numerous but we'd also identified seven Scottish-ringed birds as well as one from France and another from the Spanish translocation. Djoudj National Park, a vast wetland site in northern Senegal, proved to be one of the more productive sites for colour-ringed birds and also provided us with by far the most significant sighting of the entire trip. On 3 February – our final day at Djoudj – we spent eight hours at Lac de Gainth, sheltering from a strong easterly wind that was blowing sand direct from the Sahara. Chiffchaffs and Sedge Warblers were busy searching the marginal vegetation for food, a huge crocodile was basking on the shoreline and two African Fish Eagles sat quietly beside the lake. Then suddenly an adult female Osprey came into view. She was so close that through binoculars it was possible to see a white ring on her right leg, telling us that she was English. John Wright managed to take a few photos of her before she disappeared over our heads and out

German juvenile with Garganeys at Djoudj National Park, January 2011.

English-ringed adult female Osprey, Djoudj National Park, February 2011.

A total of 28 colour-ringed Ospreys was identified by members of the project team during field visits to West Africa in 2011 and 2012. Sixteen of the birds were from Germany, eight from Scotland and one each from England, France and Spain. There are twice as many breeding Ospreys in Germany as in Scotland so, interestingly, this ratio reflects the population size in each country.

Date first seen	Site	Country	Ring ring	Colour	Leg	Age	Year ringed	Sex	Origin
14-Jan-11	Banjul	Gam	5GZ	B/W	L	Ad	2007	♂	G
15-Jan-11	Sine-Saloum	Sen	UR	B/W	L	Ad	1999	♂	G
15-Jan-11	Sine-Saloum	Sen	SL	Bl/W	L	Juv	2010	♂	Sc
17-Jan-11	Tanji Marsh	Gam	3PV	B/W	L	Ad	2009	♂	G
20-Jan-11	Kartong	Gam	0IR	B/W	L	Ad	2006	♂	G
20-Jan-11	Kartong	Gam	3EI	B/W	L	Ad	2005	♂	G
20-Jan-11	Kartong	Gam	S79	B/W	L	Ad	2002	♀	G
20-Jan-11	Kartong	Gam	♂	O/B	L	Ad	2004	♂	F
22-Jan-11	Sine-Saloum	Sen	MP	Bl/W	L	Juv	2010	♂	Sc
22-Jan-11	Sine-Saloum	Sen	KL	W/B	L	Ad	2009	♀	Sc
22-Jan-11	Sine-Saloum	Sen	9NE	B/W	L	Juv	2010	♂	G
24-Jan-11	Tanji Marsh	Gam	LL	W/B	L	Juv	2010	♂	Sc
25-Jan-11	Tanji Marsh	Gam	UR	W/B	L	Juv	2010	♀	Sc
28-Jan-11	Djoudj	Sen	6OO	B/W	L	Ad	2009	♀	G
28-Jan-11	Djoudj	Sen	8SI	B/W	L	Juv	2010	♂	Sp
1-Feb-11	Djoudj	Sen	2OW	B/W	L	Ad	2009	♀	G
1-Feb-11	Djoudj	Sen	2ST	B/W	R	Juv	2010	♀	G
4-Feb-11	Djoudj	Sen	YU	B/W	R	Ad	2008	♀	E
7-Feb-11	Tanji Beach	Gam	9JY	B/W	L	Ad	2007	♀	G
8-Feb-11	Tanji Marsh	Gam	KY	Bl/W	L	Ad	2009	♂	Sc
8-Feb-11	Tanji Marsh	Gam	F93	B/W	R	Ad	2000	♀	G
12-Jan-12	River Allahein	Gam	0IB	B/W	L	Ad	2006	♀	G
17-Jan-12	Sine-Saloum	Sen	8GP	B/W	L	Ad	2008	♂	G
21-Jan-12	Tanji Marsh	Gam	0IX	B/W	L	Ad	2007	♀	G
21-Jan-12	Tanji Marsh	Gam	ED	Bl/W	L	Ad	2010	♀	Sc
22-Jan-12	Tanji Beach	Gam	3GM	B/W	L	Ad	2006	♂	G
25-Jan-12	Bijoli Island	Gam	CT	Bl/W	L	Ad	2009	♂	Sc
30-Jan-12	Foret de Baria	Sen	AE	Bl/W	L	Ad	2009	♂	Sc

Abbreviation key – Countries: Gam = The Gambia; Sen = Senegal. Colours: B/W = black and white; O/B = orange and black; Bl/W = blue and white. Countries of origin: G = Germany; Sc = Scotland; F = France; Sp = Spain; E = England.

of sight. Our hearts were in our mouths as he zoomed in on the photo. Could it be an Osprey from Rutland Water? We could see a 'Y' on the first photo. So far, so good. Then on the second photo we could make out the second digit. It was a 'U', meaning the bird was white/black YU. It was not one from Rutland Water, but a female ringed by Pete Davies at the Bassenthwaite nest in the Lake District in 2007. Of course we were disappointed that it wasn't a Rutland Water bird, but elated that, having travelled more than 3,000 miles from the UK, we had found an English Osprey. This was confirmed an hour later when I received a text message from Pete to say it was definitely one of the Lake District birds. Fantastic!

Another notable colour-ringed bird was one that we first saw in 2011 and then again in 2012. In March 2004 John Wright, Barrie Galpin and I visited Rolf Wahl in France. Rolf has been monitoring the expanding Osprey population in Orleans Forest for many years and it was great to spend a couple of days monitoring his newly returned birds that spring. One of the birds Rolf took us to see was an adult male with an orange ring bearing the male sign. Rolf had caught and ringed the bird as an adult in 2001 and it had bred for several years on one of his artificial nests in the forest. Imagine our delight, therefore, when we saw the same bird fishing in the River Allahein in The Gambia in 2011. John took several photos, which we sent to Rolf when we got back to the UK. He was thrilled that we'd found one of his favourite birds and promised us a bottle of champagne next time we visited him in France. Next winter, when we saw the bird again at the same spot on the River Allahein, I joked that Rolf now owed us two bottles.

During the course of the two trips to West Africa we identified a total of 29 colour-ringed birds, over half from the rapidly expanding German population and ten from Scotland. In the days of high-tech satellite tracking it showed that ringing can still be a valuable way of learning more about our migratory birds.

THE RETURN HOME

By early March adult Ospreys have been in West Africa for more than five months. We're not sure exactly what prompts them to fly north, but we do know that they are often remarkably consistent in the timing of their return to Rutland. 03(97) is usually the first bird back – on 19 or 20 March – and the remaining birds follow at predictable intervals. For experienced adult birds the flight north is usually very similar to the southward migration. The birds will often aim for the same intermediate points as they do during their autumn journey and although some may make a slightly more direct flight across the Sahara to save time, in general their routes vary little. Once the adult birds have left, life becomes much easier for the juveniles, which remain in Africa for the whole of their second calendar year. The young birds that have survived their first winter in Africa will now have honed their fishing skills and with the adults heading north, there is reduced competition for food. By the spring many of the juvenile or sub-adult birds will have settled somewhere after their winter wanderings and many will remain there for the rest of the summer. This is an important time for them; they now have a chance to get firmly established on their own patch, so that when a batch of new juveniles arrives in the autumn, they will be in a position to defend it.

By the time these young sub-adult birds start to prepare for the return flight to the UK, they will have been in West Africa for around 18 months. They often head north for the first time in April or May. While adult birds with established nests will be eager to get back as quickly as possible, there is not the same urgency for sub-adult birds. Having only made one flight south, the return migration still presents a serious challenge for them but they now have the necessary fishing skills to at least make that aspect of the journey easier. The fact that they can afford to make leisurely progress and don't need to take

unnecessary risks is also important. In many ways this first flight north is a dry run for future years, when the urge to return faster and earlier will grow stronger. Our knowledge of this first return migration is still fairly limited – satellite transmitters have only recently become reliable enough to follow the birds for a number of years – but it seems that the sub-adult birds often remain faithful to their autumn route, with refinements here and there, especially if they encountered problems on the flight south. As during the autumn journey they cross the Sahara as quickly as possible, but once they reach Europe their progress usually becomes much more leisurely. They often return to places they visited on the autumn flight and these stopover points become important intermediate points for future migrations – places where the birds know they can feed and rest.

At Rutland Water our earliest sub-adult returnees have appeared in late April, but it's more usual for them to arrive later in the summer, often in June or July. In some cases – AW(06) being a good example – we've only seen them very briefly as two-year-olds. They spend much of the summer exploring and recent satellite-tracking research suggests that young birds wander widely all over England, these exploratory flights providing valuable knowledge for the future.

Most Ospreys don't breed for the first time until they are three or four years old, so that by the time they've raised their own young they will have flown back and forth to Africa at least four times. They will now know their migration route and wintering site well and the journey becomes far less hazardous. Research in Scotland shows that 90% of adult Ospreys return each year, demonstrating that once they've survived the demanding first migration and refined their journey, things get easier. As the flights of 09(98) and AW(06) from Rutland Water really do prove, Ospreys are true master navigators.

TRACKING 09(98) HOME

As interesting as it is to follow an Osprey's autumn migration to West Africa, there is something even more exciting about being able to track Ospreys as they fly north in the spring. In March 2012 we followed a Rutland Osprey flying home for the first time.

09(98) had spent the winter on the Senegal coast, midway between Dakar and St Louis. Having arrived there in mid-September, he made only very local movements – usually less than a mile – for the next six months. He had a predictable daily routine, usually fishing just offshore once or twice each day and spending the rest of the day in one or two favoured spots, either on the beach or just inland.

Aerial view of a spectacular ridge in the Sahara. 09(98) appeared to follow this as he flew north in spring 2012.

As already discussed, we're not sure exactly what it is that triggers Ospreys to head north in the spring, but we know that they're extremely predictable in the timing of their departure – or they are if the dates they arrive back in Rutland are anything to go by. Knowing that 09(98) had arrived back on 29 March in 2011 and that his autumn migration had taken just over two weeks, we expected him to leave the Senegal coast in mid-March. And that's exactly what he did. At 1pm on 12 March he was 19 miles north of his wintering site, following the coast north-east at an altitude of nearly 1,000 metres. He was on his way home.

The year 2012 was 09(98)'s thirteenth spring migration and we, perhaps wrongly, assumed that a bird as experienced as he was would be immune to the hazards of migration, but this proved not to be the case. His flight north started easily enough. By 7pm on 12 March he had flown just under 100 miles, passing Djoudj National Park and then the Senegal River en route to southern Mauritania. That night he roosted amongst sparse vegetation with the vast wilds of the Sahara ahead of him. The previous autumn 09(98) had taken four days to cross the Sahara using a direct route through the deserts of Morocco, Western Sahara and Mauritania. It was noticeable that he used just about the most direct route possible – rather than sticking to the West African coast he headed straight across the desert, foregoing the opportunity to feed en route in order to cross the desert as quickly as possible. We expected him to do likewise on the flight north. Having paired up with 5N(04) following the disappearance of 08(97) in May the previous year, he had every reason to get back to Rutland as quickly as possible. It was a surprise, therefore, that the next morning he made a very definite change of course. After leaving his roost site sometime after 9am he headed purposefully north-west, arriving at the Mauritanian coast two hours later. This seemed a conscious decision. Perhaps he intended to follow the coast north? That certainly seemed to be the case: he continued migrating for another eight hours that day, covering 115 miles north along the coast before settling to roost 3 miles inland at 7pm. Next morning he continued on the same course and by 1pm was really motoring, flying north at 51mph at an altitude of almost 500 metres. Assuming the visibility was relatively good, it would have been easy for him to follow the coastline from this altitude. By 7pm that evening, 09(98) had flown 184 miles, the same as his daily average during his autumn migration. Next day he made similarly steady progress, flying a further 202 miles into Western Sahara and again keeping close to the coast.

So far so good – 09(98) was now more than 600 miles into the 3,000-mile journey and making steady progress north. But then things got tougher. His flight on 16 March started normally enough. He left his overnight roost in the barren deserts of Western Sahara just before 8am and headed north-west, back towards the coast. By 11am he had reached the Atlantic and for the next five hours he made steady progress north, covering just under 90 miles and again keeping staunchly to the coastline. The satellite transmitters provide us with a truly unique insight into each bird's individual migration, but they can only tell us so much. Many factors influence migration, not least the weather. 09(98)'s GPS fix at 6pm showed that he was now 5 miles off the coast at an altitude of 1,400 metres, but what we didn't know was that he was now having to contend with strong north-easterly winds. Whereas the coast of Western Sahara arcs round in a north-easterly direction, 09(98) continued to fly almost due north, the wind forcing him away from the coast. By 8pm he wasn't only having to contend with the wind, but was now flying in the dark. An hour later, when we received the last GPS fix of the day, he was halfway to the Canary Islands. For a younger, more inexperienced bird, this may have spelled the end, but at some point in the night 09(98) managed to reorientate himself. The next data we received from his transmitter – at 5am the next morning – showed that he was still over the sea, but now 80 miles due west of his position at 9pm and just 10 miles from the coast. He was now flying at a very low level – just 2 metres above the sea – in order to avoid the worst of the headwind and to utilise the updraught created by the sea.

09(98)'s close call demonstrates that there's no guarantee even the most experienced breeding Ospreys will return each spring. Migration is an extremely demanding time for the birds, irrespective of how many times they've made the journey between Africa and Rutland. We had wondered how 09(98)'s flight through the night and across the sea would affect him and, as we expected, he made slow progress once

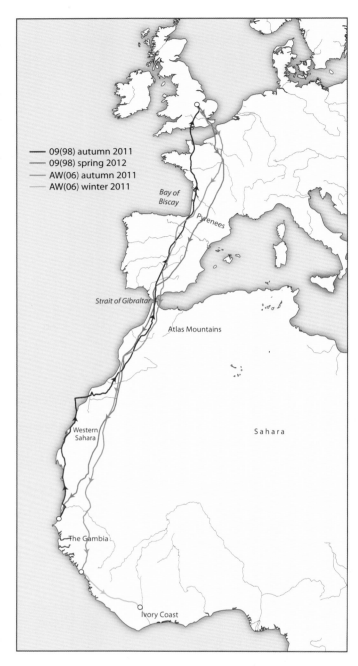

GPS satellite transmitters allowed the migrations of 09(98) and AW(06) to be tracked in remarkable detail.

beside a lake just 13 miles further north. He remained there for the rest of the day, moving only a few metres later in the evening to roost amongst sparse vegetation.

Although 09(98) was now 10 miles inland, he was still much further west than he had been on his autumn migration route. After his long flight across the sea he appeared reluctant to continue north along the coast and next day he flew 83 miles due east, before turning north again at 6pm. There is no doubt that Ospreys use prominent geographic features to help them navigate and 09(98)'s change of direction at 6pm appeared to be triggered by the sight of a spectacular ridge system that runs across the north-western edge of the Sahara. This is a ridge that other satellite-tagged birds appear to have followed in the past – and one that is easily visible from passenger aircraft over the Sahara.

Next day 09(98) continued to follow the ridge north-east. He maintained a remarkably consistent heading for the rest of the day and by 6pm he was at the southern edge of the Atlas Mountains, having flown 221 miles at altitudes of between 500 and 1,000 metres. These vast mountains present an obvious barrier to migrating birds, but sensing that he needed to press on, 09(98) continued north-east regardless, passing between peaks that rise to more than 3,000 metres. By 8pm he was clear of the mountains, but showing no signs of letting up. He continued flying for at least another three hours in complete darkness before finally settling to roost just north of Barrage Al Massira, a reservoir in northern Morocco that he had passed on his autumn migration six months earlier. He had covered 370 miles in 15 hours and now had Europe firmly in his sights.

As he approached the north coast of Africa, 09(98) was following the same course as he had on his autumn journey. He reached the coast just west of Ceuta at 3pm on 21 March and made light work of the short flight across the Mediterranean, taking less than half an hour to reach Spanish airspace, then continuing north over Algeciras and into Andalucía. By 7pm he had flown 70 miles north through Spain and was perched beside a small lake near La Puebla de Cazalla, perhaps eating a fish. Having flown 350 miles since leaving northern Morocco that morning, we expected him to settle down to roost for the night. 09(98), though, had other ideas. By 6am the next morning – when we received the next GPS fix from his transmitter – he'd reached Madrid. He had flown 225 miles across the Sierra Morena mountains in almost complete darkness; a waning crescent meant that he didn't even have moonlight to guide him. It's hard to know exactly how he navigated through the mountains; he certainly wasn't using geographical features to guide him, but there's no doubt that experience gleaned from his 75,000 miles of migrating over 13 years would have stood him in good stead. Here was an Osprey who knew exactly where he was going.

Having reached Madrid, 09(98) showed no signs of letting up. After resting for a few hours, he pressed on, flying

he was back on dry land. After a few hours' rest, he made only stuttering progress north-west, stopping regularly as he struggled to recover from the exertions of the previous 24 hours. His cause wasn't helped by the wind, which was now whipping up sandstorms in the desert. It would have been tough going for 09(98) even without his long flight over the sea, but the fact that he was now very tired must have made the flight even more arduous. By 1pm he had flown just 30 miles and he made similarly slow progress during the early part of the afternoon. In fact he only continued migrating for another two hours; at 3pm he was perched another 200 miles north before roosting in a wooded valley in the foothills of the Pyrenees, 23 miles east of Pamplona. The previous autumn 09(98) had migrated directly through the Pyrenees, but by following a more westerly course north from Madrid, he was now in a position where he could easily avoid the high peaks. Sure enough, next morning he skirted around the western edge of the mountains and into France.

Over the course of the next three days 09(98) made leisurely progress through France, following the Atlantic coast north past Bordeaux, La Rochelle and on towards Brittany, averaging just over 100 miles each day. We were surprised by his relaxed pace; his long flight through Spain had suggested he was eager to get home, but now he appeared to be taking his time. Perhaps this was a sign of fatigue after a long and arduous migration? On the evening of 25 March, 09(98) was finally within striking distance of the English Channel and chose a grand location to spend the evening – the grounds of Le Château de La Seilleray in Pays de la Loire. The satellite data suggested he may even have fished at a pond directly in front of the vast château. We wondered whether the residents noticed their overnight visitor.

We were sure 09(98) would cross the English Channel the next day, but he confounded us again by flying only 84 miles to the border of Brittany and Lower Normandy. Perhaps he would have picked up his pace if he had known what was happening in Rutland? Unbeknown to him, the female he'd paired with the previous summer – 5N(04) – was now fraternising with another male. The next day dawned sunny and clear. With only a light north-easterly breeze to contend with it was the perfect day to cross the Channel. Sure enough, 09(98) set out across the sea just before 2pm. He maintained a consistent pace of 20–25mph for the next four hours. The north-east headwind caused him to drift slightly west as he crossed the Channel, but by 6pm he was within sight of land, flying over the western part of the Isle of Wight, over the Solent Estuary and then on towards Southampton. 09(98) was not alone – numerous Ospreys were seen coming in off the sea by birdwatchers all along the south coast that day. Once north of Southampton, he turned north-east, his in-built compass directing him back towards Rutland Water. He was now eager to be home and flew for two hours after dark before roosting in farmland a few miles north-east of Winchester.

09(98) would have known he was close to home, and next morning he set off before first light. By 7am he had already flown 14 miles and was heading purposefully north. He stopped briefly at 9am, but an hour later he was another 12 miles further north-east, flying over Aylesbury. By midday he was passing Grafham Water and nearing home, maintaining a speed of between 20 and 25mph. By 2pm he would have been able to see Rutland Water from his altitude of 350 metres.

Meanwhile, John Wright and I were at 09(98)'s nest waiting for him. His migration had generated a huge amount of interest in the UK and we were determined to see him arrive

Dawn over the Pyrenees.

back at his nest. His transmitter's duty cycle meant that at the time we didn't know exactly when he would arrive so all we could do was sit and wait. Given his usual flight speeds on migration we estimated that the flight from Winchester to Rutland could take as little as four or five hours, so that he could have been back at his nest as early as 11am.

At 11.30am, a false alarm. An Osprey appeared from the south and alighted on the nest. It was 5N(04), the female 09(98) had paired up with last summer. She remained at the nest for ten minutes, adding a couple of small sticks, before heading off again. Perhaps she was just checking to see if 09(98) had returned. By lunchtime, it was a beautiful warm spring day and there were lots of signs of migration. Newly arrived Chiffchaffs were singing near the nest and a couple of groups of Fieldfare called above our heads as they flew north, back towards their Scandinavian breeding grounds.

At 2.10pm an Osprey appeared above our heads from the south. It was low down and heading straight for the nest. What's more, it flew in at such an angle that we could see a transmitter on its back. It was 09(98). He circled the nest and then folded his wings, dropping spectacularly down onto the T-perch beside the nest. He was home.

It's always a very memorable moment to see an Osprey return in this way, but the fact that we knew exactly what 09(98) had experienced over the 16 days since leaving his wintering site on the Senegal coast made it all the more

09(98) arrived back in Rutland just after 2pm on 28 March – the same day as the previous year. He spent most of the afternoon resting at Site N.

09(98) Resting in the evening
29.3.12.

09(98) arriving back from Africa at 14.10 hr. He landed on the perch next to the site N nest.
Rutland – 28-3-12.

special. He looked in fine condition and certainly displayed no adverse effects from the long and arduous journey, particularly his near-death experience off the coast of Western Sahara and his long flight through the night across Spain.

He remained at Site N for much of the day, returning with a Roach just before 5pm and advertising his arrival with a spectacular aerial display. Having followed his journey south in September, his winter in Senegal and then his return migration, the sight of him displaying above our heads against a bright blue Rutland sky was a very special moment and one I will remember for a long time.

FARID SOLVES THE MYSTERY OF 09(98)

Having captivated an audience of thousands as he migrated home to Rutland in the spring, 09(98)'s autumn migration in September 2012 was eagerly anticipated. He left Rutland on 5 September, and made excellent progress south, averaging more than 250 miles per day. By 3pm on 11 September he had reached a ridge in southern Morocco, with the vast wilds of the Sahara ahead. Sadly, though, that was as far as he got.

Over the next week we continued to receive GPS transmissions from exactly the same location on the edge of the desert suggesting that, sadly, 09(98) had probably died. The only way we could be sure was to appeal for someone to go and look. Farid Lacroix, an ex-search-and-rescue helicopter pilot, immediately offered to help. Twenty-four hours later, Farid drove five hours south from his home in Agadir and, using his GPS as a guide, trekked up a ridge in searing desert heat. As we feared, he found that 09(98) had been killed, almost certainly predated by an Eagle Owl while he roosted on the ridge. It demonstrated that, even for a master migrator like 09(98), migration is a perilous time. It was incredibly sad news, but by responding to our plea for help so quickly, Farid had highlighted how migrating birds can link people across the world. International collaboration is key to the conservation of migratory birds and we hope, in his own small way, 09(98) had helped to demonstrate that.

Volunteer Diary, Chris Ditchburn, 2011

I first became involved in the project in 2010. Having moved to the Rutland area in the summer of 2009, I attended the Birdfair, got chatting to Tim Mackrill and put my name down as a volunteer for the next Osprey season.

I have to admit to being slightly envious of those volunteers that have been involved in the project since its inception – how wonderful it must be to look back on the last 17 years and to see how far the project has come. I already have countless precious memories.

The first meeting I attended was the pre-season meet in 2010. It was in early April and I knew no one except for Tim. At the very end of the meeting there was mention of a trip to West Africa to look for colour-ringed Ospreys on their wintering grounds. What an opportunity! I eagerly approached Tim at the end of the meeting to put my name on the list. I'd just signed up for a trip to West Africa without undertaking a single shift as a volunteer, having never previously travelled outside Europe and, perhaps more importantly, without telling my wife.

I didn't regret it. That first trip to West Africa in January 2011 was amazing. I didn't know what to expect but the whole trip left a lasting impression on me that I will never forget, from the flight itself – following what could easily have been an Osprey migration route – to the sights, sounds and indeed smells of Africa. Seeing more than 35 Ospreys out in the Sine-Saloum Delta, including 14 perched on a 200-metre stretch of sandbar, was truly memorable. Seeing Ospreys going about the business of fishing just offshore from Tanji, a small fishing village in The Gambia, illustrated to us at first-hand how these wonderful birds live alongside humans when on their wintering grounds.

It's this human interaction that has led to another opportunity, and that is to visit Gambian schools as part of the project, to start forging links and educating the local children on the importance of the Ospreys and indeed all bird life – how it's important to conserve the birds and to educate the children on the importance of tourism to The Gambia, and how the rich bird life plays a part in bringing tourists to the country.

Having been twice now I look back and think, what if I hadn't gone to that volunteers meeting, and what if I hadn't taken a leap of faith and signed up for the first trip? I wouldn't have seen the Ospreys on their wintering grounds. I wouldn't have seen magnificent raptors like the Martial Eagle or Verreaux's Eagle Owls in their natural habitat, or crocodiles and baboons – the list is endless and all from the opportunity of volunteering.

Whatever your chosen hobby or passion, I encourage you to volunteer some of your time; you never know what opportunities it will open up if you do, or more importantly the opportunities you may miss if you don't.

Osprey with catfish on the Lampsar River, Northern Senegal. Feb 2011

The Legacy
of the Project

LESSONS LEARNT

When we received the licence to translocate the first Ospreys to Rutland Water in 1996, it was the green light to some ground-breaking conservation; the translocation project was the first of its kind in Europe. Similar work had been done with Ospreys in North America, but this was the first time that a translocation project involving Ospreys had been given the go-ahead this side of the Atlantic.

As Helen describes earlier in the book, the first few years of the project were a steep learning curve for all involved. The losses of the first year were a serious setback, but in hindsight they resulted in some positive changes. We quickly realised that translocating runt chicks, which were more prone to disease than healthier ones, was not a sensible idea. Translocating larger, healthier individuals – who were more robust and better able to look after themselves – combined with improved hygiene and day-to-day care, meant that of the 67 chicks translocated between 1997 and 2005, all were released successfully and all except two survived to migration. Meanwhile back in Scotland, the adult Ospreys at donor nests proved far more effective than us at rearing smaller, weaker chicks. By removing one chick from broods of two or three we actually enhanced the remaining chicks' chances of survival, particularly if there was a runt in the nest. Moving the release pens to Lax Hill was significant too. In the first year, when the cages were situated close to the lagoons, dense vegetation surrounding them caused problems when the youngsters were released. The subsequent move to a more elevated, open release site made the birds' all-important first flights less hazardous and, importantly, easier to monitor.

In hindsight, the one mistake we made was not releasing more females. Evidence from the USA suggested that, because males are generally more inclined to breed closer to their natal site than females, we should translocate more male chicks. However, releasing three times as many males as females – 49 males compared to just 16 females between 1996 and 2001 – probably resulted in a much slower population expansion than if we'd released a 50:50 split. It would appear that in the early years, the presence of a few inexperienced males on nests was not enough to persuade passing Scottish females to stay and breed, as the original project rationale predicted. Now, with a small breeding colony established, the area appears much more alluring to passing females – in 2011 three of the five breeding females were non-Rutland birds – but that wasn't the case in the early years. We were fortunate that a single pair of translocated birds, 03(97) and 05(00), was so prolific, raising 17 chicks between 2003 and 2008. Several of their offspring have now returned to breed themselves, and they in turn have attracted immigrant birds from other populations. This has given the Rutland colony a much-needed boost and, if the expansion of the Scottish population is anything to go by, we should start to see a dramatic population increase in the coming years.

The prediction that the rate of population growth will increase over time is given more credence by the return rate of wild-fledged Rutland birds. Of the 75 birds that were translocated between 1996 and 2005, ten returned to Rutland Water, with eight breeding successfully. This is comparable to the North American translocations, but considerably less than the return rate of wild-fledged Rutland chicks. By the end of summer 2012, 16 wild-fledged chicks had made it back to Rutland, giving a return rate of 37%, significantly more than that of translocated birds (13%). This bodes well for the future

Birds translocated to Rutland

Year	Number of birds translocated	Number surviving to migration	Number returning	Number breeding
1996	8	4	0	0
1997	8	8	2♂ (+ 1♂ to Wales)	2♂ (+ 1♂ in Wales)
1998	12	12	2♂ (+ 1♂ to Wales)	2♂ (+ 1♂ in Wales)
1999	12	12	0 (+ 1♂ to Scotland)	0 (+ 1♀ bred in Scotland)
2000	12	12	2♂ and 1♀	1♂ and 1♀
2001	12	11	2♂ and 1♀	1♂ and 1♀
2005	11	10	0	0

Breeding Ospreys in Rutland

Year	Number of breeding pairs	Number of young fledged	Number of young returning to Rutland colony in future years	Number of translocated birds breeding	Number of Rutland-fledged birds breeding	Number of Scottish or unringed birds breeding
2001	1	1	0	1♂		1♀
2002	1	0	0	1♂		1♀
2003	2	5	0	2♂ and 2♀		
2004	1	2	2	1♂ and 1♀		
2005	1	3	2	1♂ and 1♀		
2006	1	3	1	1♂ and 1♀		
2007	2	5	0	2♂ and 1♀	1♀	
2008	3	3	1	3♂ and 1♀	1♀	1♀
2009	4	9	4	4♂	2♀	2♀
2010	5	12	6	3♂	2♂ and 2♀	3♀
2011	5	10	?	3♂	2♂ and 2♀	3♀
2012	4	9	?	3♂	1♂ and 2♀	2

growth of the colony, especially given the number of young now fledging from nests in the area each year.

As shown in the tables above, the return rate for both translocated and wild-fledged birds varies considerably between years. Whereas a total of six of the 24 juveniles released in 2000 and 2001 returned to Rutland, none of the birds translocated in 1996, 1999 or 2005 returned to the area. While the lack of returnees from the first year of the translocation was not unexpected, we were surprised that none of the birds released in 1999 or 2005 returned to Rutland Water. By 1999 we had refined the translocation techniques and all birds appeared to leave Rutland in good condition. Likewise in 2005, although the 'top-up' translocation was biased in favour of females – which are less site-faithful – we expected at least one or two birds to return, given return rates in previous years. A similar pattern is true of the wild-fledged birds. For instance, both of the juveniles that fledged in 2004 and six of the 12 that flew south in 2012 returned, but none of the juveniles from 2003 or 2007 – five chicks each year – were seen again in Rutland. It seems likely that weather conditions on migration and the availability of good-quality fishing sites in Africa are the most likely explanation for this variation. For instance, strong easterly winds in early September may lead to years when more birds are lost in the Bay of Biscay and, in years with lower than average rainfall in the West African rainy season, there will be reduced foraging opportunities for the juveniles when they first arrive on the wintering grounds.

Although the return rate of translocated birds to Rutland is considerably less than that of the wild-fledged individuals, the positive benefits of the translocation cannot be overstated. The eight translocated birds that have reared young have successfully established a Rutland colony and it's their returning offspring that are now key to the future growth of the population. Were it not for translocation, central England would not have breeding Ospreys. Our work has shown that restoring a population of Ospreys through translocation, though far more difficult than for both Red Kites and White-tailed Eagles, is possible. It's not just in central England, though, that the translocation has had an influence.

THE VALUE OF TRANSLOCATION – CHANGING DISTRIBUTIONS

When we began the project in 1996 our long-term aim was not just to establish a breeding population of Ospreys in Rutland – we also hoped to restore these very special birds to a large part of southern Britain. If you were to travel 400 years back in time you'd see Ospreys throughout England and Wales – numerous historical documents suggest that the birds were widespread throughout the UK and probably a very familiar part of the English countryside. This is emphasised by the fact that Shakespeare refers to Ospreys in *The Tragedy of Coriolanus*: 'He'll be to Rome as is the Osprey to the fish, who takes it by sovereignty of nature.' If Shakespeare was using Ospreys as a metaphor, then he must have thought that most people in that era would have

known what one was, or why else mention them? By moving the birds to Rutland Water we hoped that we could establish a population in central England and that, in time, the birds would spread to other parts of southern Britain. What we didn't expect was that it would happen as quickly as it did.

In June 2004 we received some startling news. A pair of breeding Ospreys had been found in North Wales, close to the small town of Porthmadog on the edge of Snowdonia. Sadly their nest had collapsed after a prolonged spell of bad weather, killing their two chicks, but the two adult birds had remained on territory. More significantly than that, the male had an orange ring on his right leg. There was every chance it was a bird from Rutland Water. Up until that point no one had been able to read the ring so John, Barrie Galpin and I offered to travel over in early July to see if we could solve the mystery.

We were met by local resident Steve Watson. Steve had found the nest earlier in the year and was as keen to know the identity of the male bird as we were. He led us to the spot where he'd been watching the birds for the past month or so. Although much of the nest had been lost, the remaining sticks were precariously positioned in the top of

11(98) has bred at a nest in the Glaslyn Valley in North Wales every year since 2004. He was not seen at Rutland Water after his first migration in 1998, having been translocated from northern Scotland that year.

Streaked throat breast

Extremely dark

♀ sketched from a long distance away so head pattern might not be accurate

slight hint of an eye brow but very faint

♂

orange 11 on right leg – A 1998 ♂ Rutland bird!

A few central spots to breast

a tall Scots Pine, nestled in the beautiful Glaslyn Valley. The skyline was dominated by several of the highest Snowdonian peaks – it was certainly a spectacular spot for a nest. We quickly located the two adult birds and straight away could see the orange ring on the male's right leg. Needing to get closer if we were going to read the ring, John and I inched our way towards the bird. Using a ditch as cover we managed to get within about 250 metres, just about close enough to read the ring. As is often the case the bird was perched on one leg – not the one we wanted to see. After what seemed like an eternity it finally put its right leg down and we could read the inscription. John and I both agreed – it was orange/black 11(98), a male bird we had translocated to Rutland Water in 1998. We were thrilled, but this went against all our original predictions – all the evidence from Scotland and elsewhere suggested that males nearly always return to their natal site to breed. But here was a male who was now breeding 200 miles west of his natal site. When 11(98) hadn't returned to Rutland Water, we assumed that he'd died; it was fantastic that we now knew otherwise. Despite the fact that the nest had failed, it was encouraging that he had found a mate. She was an amazing-looking bird – her broad, dark breast markings contrasting greatly with the white breast of the male. As she was unringed we assumed that she was a Scottish bird. Although the nest had failed we hoped they would be back next spring. The nest's location, just a few miles from the rich fishing grounds of the Glaslyn Estuary, meant that in the future this could become a very productive nest site.

We spent the rest of the day with Steve, talking about Osprey conservation and the work he could do to try and attract more Ospreys to this part of Wales. There was no doubt this could be a very good area for the birds and if Steve built some artificial nests, there was every chance he would entice more breeding pairs. We also talked about how he should rebuild the original nest in order to ensure that there was no repeat of the summer's sad events.

After leaving Steve, rather than heading back to Rutland Water we drove south to Mid Wales where there was yet more exciting news. Soon after Steve had found the nest on the Glaslyn, Clive Faulkner and his colleagues at the

In 2004 07(97) raised a single chick at a nest in Mid Wales with a Scottish-ringed female. Like 11(98), he had not been seen at Rutland Water since his first migration. Sadly, neither 07(97) nor his mate returned to the nest in 2005.

Montgomeryshire Wildlife Trust received reports from local birdwatchers that they too had found a nest. And they were right – another pair of Ospreys was breeding and, unlike the Glaslyn birds, it had a healthy chick in the nest. Even more significantly, the male was another Rutland Water translocated bird. 07(97) was one of eight young Ospreys translocated in 1997 and, like 11(98), we hadn't seen him back at the reservoir since he set off on his first migration. He had paired up with a female that had originally fledged from a nest on the Black Isle in north-east Scotland. Sadly 07(97) was not at the nest – in a dead larch tree in the middle of a large arable field – while we were at the nest with Clive, but it was great to see his mate and chick on the nest.

So what was going on? Male Ospreys are usually highly site-faithful, but now, quite unexpectedly, we had two translocated males breeding in Wales, some 200 miles west of Rutland Water. Neither bird had been seen at Rutland Water since its first migration but that didn't mean they hadn't dropped in briefly. We know that young Rutland Water birds wander widely all over southern parts of the UK when they first return as two-year-olds, so there was every chance they may have returned to Rutland Water at some point. If this was the case, why hadn't they stayed? Of course we'll never know for sure, but it's interesting that the Welsh nests are on the same latitude as Rutland Water. The point was, in the space of a few years, the Rutland translocation had completely changed the Osprey distribution map in the UK, and that was really exciting news. If the birds could get established in Wales then, clearly, the population in southern Britain would expand faster, both geographically and numerically.

The problem with having a few isolated pairs is that if one of the breeding birds doesn't return, it's far more difficult for the lone bird to find a new mate than in an established colony where there is often a plethora of unattached young birds. Although 11(98) and his mate returned to Glaslyn and bred successfully in 2005, 07(97) and his Scottish mate did not. Or perhaps more likely, one of them did not. Whatever the case, 2004 was the only year that particular nest was used. Fortunately 11(98) has been much more successful and has now raised a total of 21 chicks with the same unringed female at Glaslyn. Several of his offspring have returned and one of them, a male, first bred near Threave in southern Scotland in 2009. Like his father, he had chosen to nest some 200 miles from his natal site.

If it was surprising that the two translocated males had bred in Wales in 2004, events in 2011 were more expected, but just as exciting. By 2011 three unringed females were breeding in Rutland and this backed up research that has shown that female Ospreys are more inclined to nest away from their natal site than males. We wondered how long it would be before one of our Rutland females nested elsewhere.

In 2007 the Montgomeryshire Wildlife Trust erected an Osprey nest platform on its Cors Dyfi reserve near Machynlleth. Various Ospreys, including wandering birds from Glaslyn, were seen at the nest almost straightaway. Then in 2009 an unringed male, later to become known as Monty, took up residence at the nest. Despite the fact that he failed to attract a mate for either of the next two summers, his presence at the nest raised hopes that Mid Wales might have breeding Ospreys once again. In spring 2011 Monty returned to the nest in early April. A few days later he was joined by a female. Project Manager Emyr Evans, a friend of the Rutland Water team, immediately noticed that the female had a white ring on her right leg. Realising the significance

03(08) on the Cors Dyfi nest in Mid Wales. She was not seen back at Rutland Water following her first migration in 2008.

of this – Emyr had previously managed the Glaslyn site for the RSPB – he was extremely excited. The fact that the bird was ringed on the right leg meant that she was either Welsh or English. Although Emyr's nest cameras were not yet working, wildlife photographer Gary Ridsdale came to the rescue. Gary, by chance, was visiting the nest the day after the female arrived and was able to get several good-quality photos of her. It turned out that she was another of 03(97)'s progeny: 03(08), a female who had fledged from Site B at Rutland Water in 2008.

03(08), or Nora as she later became known, had not been seen at Rutland Water since her first migration in autumn 2008. That year John Wright had been at the Site B nest when she set out on migration and, as it turned out, that was the last time any of us would see her in Rutland. Two years later, in 2010, she may have made a fleeting visit to the Dyfi nest – her white ring caught on camera – but, unlike some of the other young females we've seen at Rutland Water, she didn't pair up with Monty that summer.

Nora's arrival at Cors Dyfi in April 2011 was followed by three weeks of courtship before she laid her first egg. The usual nervous period then followed for the Dyfi team as it waited for the eggs to hatch. To add to the excitement, millions of people from all over the UK were now engrossed thanks to BBC's *Springwatch*, which was following the birds' progress. Being first-time breeders, there was no guarantee the eggs would hatch, but in early June the nest cameras captured the moment when the first chick began breaking out of its shell. All three eggs hatched within a few days. For the first time in over 400 years the Dyfi Valley had breeding Ospreys again, thanks, in no small part, to the Rutland Osprey Project.

The fact that three Rutland birds have now bred successfully in Wales, at three different sites, demonstrates what a positive impact the translocation project has had on the distribution of Ospreys in southern Britain. There would be no breeding Ospreys in Wales were it not for our work at Rutland Water and this really does show the value of positive, proactive conservation. We're now working with farmers, landowners and conservation organisations around the country to erect artificial nests in as many locations as possible. Of the five pairs that nested in the Rutland Water area in 2010, four were on the artificial nests we built. The Montgomeryshire Wildlife Trust has also shown that erecting artificial nests can have very quick results. If Rutland birds settle to breed in Wales, then there is every chance that they will colonise other parts of southern Britain far quicker than we'd hoped. In 2011 a two-year-old Rutland bird spent several weeks in Hampshire and we know from satellite tracking that sub-adults wander all over Britain before settling down to breed. The construction of new reservoirs and flooding of gravel pits has created much

03(97) and a Red Kite at Site B. Kites will sometimes attempt to steal fish from the Ospreys.

favourable Osprey habitat in the south and this, combined with numerous fish-rich river estuaries, has resulted in great potential for the birds to spread through England, Wales and beyond, especially if artificial nests are erected. At Rutland Water definite hierarchies exist, so that when young male birds return for the first time, they are chased away from the best sites. If they subsequently find a well-positioned artificial nest away from Rutland Water where they don't get this same hassle from older, established birds, it may persuade them to set up territory there.

By far the quickest way of restoring the birds to other parts of the south, however, would be to carry out further translocations. Red Kites have now been released at more than a dozen locations around the UK and this has had an extremely positive impact on their distribution. Twenty-five years ago birdwatchers had to make the pilgrimage to Mid Wales to stand a chance of seeing these majestic raptors, but now they're a common sight across much of the country. It's difficult to drive along the lanes of Rutland without seeing them, and perhaps more significantly, the birds are regularly seen floating leisurely above towns and cities in several parts of England. Red Kites, like Ospreys, are slow to spread naturally – they too like to breed close to their natal sites – but by releasing birds at so many locations around the country this problem has been negated. It would seem sensible, proactive conservation to do something similar with Ospreys. If Ospreys were released in Norfolk or Suffolk and then at a site somewhere on the south coast – perhaps in Hampshire or Sussex – it would completely change the UK distribution of the species. Our work at Rutland Water has shown that southern Britain is a better place for Ospreys than the remote Scottish lochs they've become synonymous with. Food is readily available and there are generally not the extremes of weather often experienced in northern Scotland. The productivity of the Rutland population – currently 2.04 – is certainly significantly higher than the corresponding figure for the population in north-east Scotland. Furthermore, research by Roy Dennis has shown that birds returning to his study area in north-east Scotland are not able to breed as early as their counterparts in the south (Dennis, 2008). Intense competition for mates and nests in areas that have reached carrying capacity results in young birds often having to wait several years before a site becomes vacant, thereby allowing them to breed. If birds were moved from these 'full-up' areas in northern Scotland to England, where there is not the same competition for nests, it would allow them to breed at a younger age. In doing so, the UK population would increase at a faster rate both numerically and geographically. Of course there are always those who say that conservation effort should not be invested in a species, such as the Osprey, with such a wide global distribution. But the point is that the only reason Ospreys are not common in southern Britain is because of the influence of man. Now that we've refined the translocation techniques, we have shown that the birds can be restored to parts of their former range relatively easily and cost-effectively. Furthermore, by re-establishing the birds in areas where they were once common we're restoring part of our lost wildlife heritage. The sight of Red Kites lazily floating over Oxford is something that people would have seen hundreds of years ago. Now, thanks to proactive conservation, it's something that people can enjoy once again. It's exciting to think that in years to come people may be able to see Ospreys fishing in the River Thames in central London. The birds from Rutland Water will eventually spread that far south, but by translocating birds to other sites, it could happen much more quickly.

ITALY

One of the most rewarding aspects of the Rutland Osprey Project is knowing that our work is having a legacy elsewhere. One of the best examples of this is in Italy. In recent centuries the persecution of Ospreys has not just been restricted to the UK – 300 years ago the birds would have been widespread throughout Europe, but persecution combined with habitat loss and the misuse of pesticides has resulted in a much more disjointed distribution. But happily, several of the European populations – including the ones in Germany and France – are now on the increase again. Many of the expanding populations around Europe have been helped by the erection of artificial nests, but translocation is now having a significant impact too. In 2003 a licence was granted to translocate Ospreys to southern Spain from Germany, Scotland and Finland. Then, soon afterwards, Italian conservationists working in Tuscany also became interested. Giampiero Sammuri, former President of the Maremma Regional Park, contacted Roy Dennis to discuss the idea of translocating Ospreys to Maremma Regional Park on the Tuscany coast. Roy was very keen and went out to Italy to give his expert opinion on the proposed release site and to discuss some of the practical aspects of a translocation. He suggested that it would be a good idea for Andrea Sforzi, scientific coordinator of the project, to visit us at Rutland Water, where we were carrying out the extra top-up translocation. By the time of Andrea's visit in August 2005, the translocated youngsters had been released, but it was good for him and his colleagues to see the release site and to discuss the refinements we'd made to the way in which we cared for and monitored the birds.

Having visited Rutland, Andrea invited myself and Barrie Galpin out to Italy that September to have a look at their potential release site. The spot they had chosen was a good one. It was located in an area of scattered Stone Pines, well protected from the strong Mediterranean sun, but providing a nice open area in front of the pens for the young birds to make their first flights. A few hundred metres from the release pens was the Ombrone River, which flowed out to the crystal-clear blue sea. It was a great location and one that we thought would be a success. The Italians had already seen Ospreys regularly on passage and had erected several artificial nests in the marsh behind the release site. While Barrie and I were there we saw an unringed female, perhaps a bird from Finland. Italy lies on the Ospreys' eastern flyway in Europe, so that breeding birds from places such as Finland, Estonia and Russia pass through Maremma each year. Historical data, however, suggest that the birds that formerly bred in Maremma were in fact more closely related to their near-neighbours in Corsica. One hundred years ago Ospreys were fairly widespread around the Mediterranean, breeding

The release pens at Maremma Regional Park in Italy, where Corsican Ospreys were first released in 2006.

along the Italian, Corsican and Sardinian coasts, with birds probably moving between the various sub-populations. By the 1950s, however, they had disappeared from mainland Italy, and by the end of the 1960s from Sicily and Sardinia too. At the beginning of the 1970s only a handful of pairs persisted in Corsica.

It's only in the comparatively recent past that the Corsican population has become more stable again, thanks to an intense conservation effort and the creation of the Scandola Marine Reserve. Somewhere in the region of 25–30 pairs nest on spectacular sea cliffs, quite unlike the traditional Scottish sites we more readily associate the birds with in the UK. They also differ in the fact that, like the few other isolated Mediterranean populations, they are relatively sedentary. Little is known about their movements in the winter, but it's believed that they don't disperse far from their breeding sites. It's also thought that they might be genetically distinct from the northern European population. Because the IUCN reintroduction criterion stipulates that, genetically, the individuals chosen for translocation must be as similar as possible to the original population, it was important that the Maremma translocation involved birds from Corsica.

In spring 2006 we heard the good news that Andrea had received a licence to translocate six birds from Corsica. He was keen for John Wright and I to help with the release and arranged for us to fly out there once the birds were ready to go.

We arrived at Maremma on a swelteringly hot day, but there was no time to enjoy the Mediterranean sun. Like us, Andrea thought it sensible to fit radio transmitters to the juveniles before their release. This had proved to be invaluable at Rutland Water during the birds' first few days on the wing; we saved several individuals from certain death by being able to locate them on the ground using the radio-tracking equipment. The transmitters are glued to the bird's central tail feather and, over the years at Rutland Water, we discovered that it's essential to do this as close to the release date as possible. If the transmitter is fitted while the feather is still growing – and has blood in the shaft – then it will nearly always fall off. The problem with this is that it's necessary to go into the pens and catch the birds the day before they are released – at which point they are more than capable of flying. Despite the fact that we were now experienced at this, it was with a certain amount of trepidation that John and I entered the pens in Maremma that afternoon. Using large towels to keep the birds calm we managed the task fairly easily, and more importantly, without injury. It was then a case of fitting the transmitters as quickly as possible; as ever, it was important to minimise human contact and to keep stress to an absolute minimum. Once the two birds that were ready for release had been fitted with their transmitters we put them back in the pens with fresh fish and left them overnight. Little did they know they were to be given their freedom next morning.

A young Osprey prepares for its first flight at Maremma.

Newly released translocated Ospreys on an artificial nest at Maramma Regional Park. The project got the go-ahead following the success of the Rutland Project.

The next day, on another beautiful sunny morning, we were at the release site early. We'd expected a media frenzy but as it turned out there was just one television camera there to record the historic event. John and I positioned ourselves in our 4×4 in front of the release pens and waited. Release day is always a nervous time and especially so when you are there to ensure all goes smoothly.

As the warden slowly lowered the fronts of the cages – just as we had done at Rutland Water many times before – the two birds sat unperturbed at the front of the pen. Suddenly they had a much clearer view of the world. Both looked out inquisitively, moving their heads from side to side in owl-like fashion. How long would it take them to pluck up the courage to fly? At Rutland Water some birds flew within a matter of minutes while others waited much longer, sometimes more than 24 hours. As we waited rollers and Great Spotted Cuckoos flew past the release pens. We didn't have that pleasure at Rutland Water. Then suddenly, almost without warning, one of the Ospreys was off. It had flapped a few times but gave no indication it was about to take the plunge. Uneasy in the air at first the youngster soon got the hang of things and completed several short circuits above the release pens. It then made a beeline for the artificial nest behind us. It was just as well it did because just as it landed it was mobbed by an Eleonora's Falcon – a large powerful falcon that breeds around the Mediterranean. The young Osprey skilfully

managed to avoid the dive from the falcon and landed safely on the nest – sighs of relief from all of us. So far, so good.

The other youngster was altogether more reluctant to leave the safety of the pens. Although alone for the first time and having watched its companion, it showed no signs of wanting to follow suit. It steadfastly refused to move. In fact for the next few hours, while the free-flying juvenile made increasingly competent flights, it barely moved from the perch at the front of the pen.

By early afternoon we were still waiting, but now a stiff breeze had developed. This was good news – once the juveniles feel wind in their feathers and the updraft their vast wingspan can produce, they often become much more active. Sure enough, the youngster began lifting off the perch and hovering above it. Suddenly it seemed that he could go at any time. After one or two abortive attempts – where he hovered above the perch for several seconds without quite mustering the courage to leave the pens – he finally made a minute-long flight just after 2pm, landing with a bit of a bump on the artificial nest next to his compatriot.

Once the birds are flying, the next big step is for them to feed. At a natural nest, the youngsters simply have to return to the nest for food, but for the translocated juveniles things are slightly less straightforward. They must learn to go and feed on fish placed on trays on or near the release pens. It often took the Rutland Water birds several days to master this

Radio tracking the released Ospreys at Maremma.

*In 2011 a pair of Ospreys raised two chicks at Maramma Regional Park –
the first successful Osprey nest in mainland Italy for over 50 years.*

*Second-calendar-year Ospreys at Diaccia Botrona Marsh, June 2007.
At this age the two males were showing no signs of aggression towards
each other.*

so, despite the fact that the two released juveniles still hadn't
fed by evening, we told Andrea, Flavio Monti (at that time
a university student collecting data for his Bachelor's thesis)
and the rest of the team not to worry. Sure enough, next day
both juveniles fed well. It had been a flawless release and we
were delighted. If the rest of the project went this smoothly,
Andrea and the team could be very happy. A few days later
the remaining juveniles were given their freedom too and
Flavio set about the task of monitoring their daily movements.

John and I went back to Maremma in 2007, when a
further eight young birds were released. To be honest we were
a little surplus to requirements – with a year's experience
the team now really knew what it was doing – but it was
fascinating to see how things were developing. It was
particularly interesting to follow the progress of the sub-adult
birds, which as predicted, had not migrated. Two of them
spent the winter at Diaccia Botrona Marsh, a few miles from
the Maremma Regional Park. They were still there when
we visited and Andrea kindly took us to see them. As young
sub-adults they still hadn't become territorial and it was great
to see the two of them sitting together on an artificial nest.

By summer 2008 things had really started to progress
well. When I arrived in late June, Flavio had already released
several birds and they were spending their time close to
the release pens. As we walked to the monitoring spot one
morning an Osprey began displaying over our heads. The
shrill display call was something I was used to hearing at
Rutland Water, but this was the first time that Flavio had
seen one of the Maremma birds displaying. We were both
absolutely thrilled. This was a sure sign that A1 and I1 were
becoming more territorial and suggested that it would not be
too long before they established territories of their own.

Over the course of the next two summers Andrea and the
team translocated another 14 birds. By spring 2011 several
of the translocated birds had reached breeding age, and there
seemed every chance that for the first time in over 50 years,
Italy would have breeding Ospreys again. Sure enough, in
April I received exciting news from Andrea. A male had been
joined by an unringed female – perhaps one from Corsica,
or maybe a migrant bird from Finland – at the Maremma
nest and they were incubating. Fantastic! The male had a
metal ring on its left leg but no colour ring, suggesting that

either A1 or I1 had lost theirs; it seemed highly unlikely that it would be any other male. We kept our fingers crossed that the nest would be successful.

As hatching time approached Andrea, Flavio and their artist friend Alessandro Troisi kept a close eye on the nest. The expected hatching date passed with no noticeable change in behaviour, but then just as everyone was starting to worry, Flavio and Alessandro witnessed the magical moment when the female offered fish down into the nest for the first time. I spoke to Flavio and Andrea later that day to congratulate them. I was delighted for many reasons, not least because it showed that our work in Rutland was now having a legacy much further afield. It was also very satisfying that one of the breeding birds was one that we had helped release that first year.

The Wow Factor, in Rutland and Further Afield

There are few more engaging birds than Ospreys. With a breeding population now established in Rutland, thousands of people travel from all over the UK every year to see them at the nature reserve. They are becoming synonymous with Rutland and increasingly important for the local economy. Significantly, not all of the people who come to see the Ospreys at Rutland Water would label themselves as birders, and this emphasises the vital role that charismatic birds such as these can play in conservation and environmental education.

In many ways the forerunner for the kind of ecotourism we now have at places like Rutland Water was George Waterstone. In 1959 Waterstone made the momentous decision to make public the location of the only pair of breeding Ospreys in Scotland. He felt that making the general public aware of the Ospreys might help deter egg collectors from raiding the nest. Little did he know that the model he developed at Loch Garten would later be copied around the UK and further afield. Not in his wildest dreams could he have predicted that 50 years later, people would be watching nesting Peregrines in central London, Red Kites over Oxford and Ospreys in the heart of England.

Peregrines have adapted superbly to our urban environment, and in years to come we hope that Ospreys will become an increasingly common sight in densely populated southern Britain. In the UK Ospreys are synonymous with remote Scottish lochs and wild places, but this is only because of persecution. The killing of Ospreys over several centuries has resulted in them becoming fearful of humans, and therefore restricted to remote places. However, if you consider where Ospreys breed in North America, things could and should be very different. In the States there is not the same history of persecution and Ospreys readily nest alongside people – in back gardens and in some cases on the masts of boats. As time progresses we hope that the birds breeding in England – where they are exposed to human contact far more often than in some of the remote parts of Scotland – will become far more tolerant and therefore more inclined to nest close to people.

There is no doubt that the presence of birds of prey adds greatly to people's enjoyment of the countryside. As already discussed earlier in this chapter a Sunday afternoon walk in Rutland will often be rewarded by the sight of a Red Kite lazily floating overhead. The reintroduction of this species has undoubtedly restored something that has been missing from our countryside for centuries. The same is true of Ospreys. We already know that most people in Shakespeare's time would have been very familiar with Ospreys, and it would be a wonderful legacy for the project if that were to be the case again. They will never become as common as Red Kites, but we've estimated that the UK could support as many as 2,000 pairs of breeding Ospreys. When you consider that the population currently stands at less than 250 pairs, there is still a long way to go.

When we began the translocation project in 1996 it generated a huge amount of interest. As the first birds arrived in July they were met by television crews from around the UK. Since then, the level of media interest in Ospreys has not waned and this high public profile means that birders and non-birders alike are always keen to hear the latest Osprey news.

Although there was always public interest in the birds, it was the advent of two things that really sparked the imagination. The first was satellite tracking. I always find that when I give talks to clubs and societies around the country, it's migration that really interests people. Satellite tracking has helped to unravel the mystery of migration and, significantly, brought it to a wide and diverse audience.

In 1999, when we tracked four of the Rutland juveniles for the first time, it was decided that this information should be presented 'live' on our newly created website. More than a decade later, with iPhones, iPads and the like, such instant information is never far from our fingertips, but in the late 1990s it was all very new and exciting. Barrie Galpin was given the job of developing the website. Barrie set up pages for each satellite-tagged bird, allowing people all around the globe to follow its progress. Each day, as new data arrived, Barrie would locate each bird's position using his atlas – there was no Google Earth in those days – and post it on the web. The level of interest was incredible. Barrie, Helen and the team quickly began to receive correspondence from all over the world. If a bird went missing or stopped off at one particular place for any length of time, people would

Fishing boats at Tanji Beach, The Gambia.

look for it. If we had a question on weather patterns or the geography of a certain area, people would email in with really useful information. It was fantastic.

Eleven years later, with the advent of the new high-tech GPS transmitters, we began to post even more detailed descriptions of the birds' migrations. As 09(98) and AW(06) flew south in 2011 we received data from their transmitters every hour. Whereas ten years previously we had sometimes gone days without signals from the transmitters, now we knew how many hours a day the birds were flying, their altitude and speed, where they were stopping off to fish and even the tree they were roosting in. With social networking sites like Facebook and Twitter all the rage it opened up the data to a whole new audience. AW(06) even got a mention on BBC Radio 2.

Our tracking of 09(98) and AW(06) also gave added impetus to a project that we'd initiated during our visit to West Africa in 2011. During the trip the team and I visited Tanji School in The Gambia. As we chatted to a class of around 30 children, it again emphasised how charismatic birds like Ospreys are vital to conservation. Many of the children's fathers were fishermen and, as a result, some had

seen Ospreys. This was not surprising: a few days later as we walked through the mass of people waiting for the boats to return to Tanji Beach with their daily catch, we watched three Ospreys fishing very close to the shore. One juvenile bird plucked a fish just a few metres from a fishing boat. There could be few better examples of how the lives of the birds are intertwined with those of humans. Although some of the class recognised Ospreys, they had no concept – and nor did some of their teachers – of the migration that the birds undertake every year. They were oblivious to the fact that the Ospreys they see fishing off Tanji Beach fly 3,000 miles each spring to breed in northern Europe.

Later that day I discussed the visit with our guide, Junkung Jadama. We agreed that for conservation of migratory species to succeed, the human communities they live alongside need to know more about them. It was clear from our visit to Tanji School that teaching people about Ospreys is a great way to raise the profile of migratory birds in West Africa, so Junkung and I agreed to initiate an education programme for schools in The Gambia. And it wasn't just in West Africa that we thought we could make a difference. Migrating birds such as Ospreys cross numerous religious, cultural and political boundaries and, as such, provide a unique opportunity to link communities. When we did the first satellite tracking in 1999 Tim Appleton had the exciting idea of linking schools along the Ospreys' migratory flyways. Now we had the opportunity to do it. Back in Rutland Michelle Househam began developing an extensive schools programme, which proved an instant hit. Like in Tanji we immediately found that Ospreys could be key to getting children interested in wildlife. Michelle and I discussed the twinning idea with Rob Gooding, head of Whissendine and St Nicholas Primary Schools. Rob thought it was a really exciting idea and agreed to link his two schools with Tanji. In December 2011 the children at Whissendine and St Nicholas wrote letters about their lives in Rutland and the Ospreys that breed just a few miles away. They also collected old football shirts as gifts for their new

friends in The Gambia. The team and I delivered the letters and football shirts when we visited Tanji a month later. It was fantastic that two communities separated by more than 3,000 miles and many other cultural differences now had something in common and a way of building relationships – through the Osprey. Since then the idea has grown and we've linked more schools along the Ospreys' migration flyway – from northern Scotland to West Africa. Schools on the eastern flyway – from Finland through Eastern Europe, the Middle East and East Africa – are also keen to join the project. We believe that this kind of international cooperation is essential to future conservation. Now, when the children from Tanji are walking along the beach, or out in boats with their fathers, perhaps they will view the Ospreys in a totally new way. Hopefully it will make them value and respect their wildlife more than they did before.

Tim Mackrill and Junkung Jadama with children at Tanji Lower Basic School watching a video message sent by pupils at Whissendine Primary School.

Tim Mackrill and Junkung Jadama with staff and pupils from Tanji Lower Basic School wearing football shirts donated by children at two Rutland primary schools.

Closer to home, the next thing to really engage with the public was breeding Ospreys in Rutland. The first nesting pair again created national headlines. It showed that proactive conservation – and let's face it, there are few things more proactive than reintroductions – really can work. More pertinently, it meant that there were now breeding Ospreys in the heart of central England, and therefore within easy reach of millions of people. A bird that was synonymous with remote, wild places was now nesting in rural England once again.

Unsurprisingly, people immediately wanted to come and see the breeding Ospreys. The problem we had was that the nest was on private farmland with no public access. It would have been great to allow people to visit Site B, but this wasn't possible. Visitors to the reservoir did have the opportunity to come and see one of our other newly returned translocated birds. 08(97) was now firmly established on territory in Manton Bay and thousands of people were able to watch his attempts to attract a female. Unfortunately, sightings could never be guaranteed. He would remain faithful to the nest throughout the spring, but once it was clear that it was too late for him to breed, he began wandering further afield in Rutland. It got us thinking that perhaps we needed to think of another way to show people Ospreys in Rutland.

There are few more dramatic sights than an Osprey diving to catch a fish. It came as no surprise, therefore, that we were often asked where was the best place to see fishing Ospreys around the reservoir. It was a good question. The reservoir encompasses 17 miles of shoreline and more than 3,100 acres of water. The Ospreys favour various areas, but there was no one spot where we could guarantee sightings of fishing Ospreys. Perhaps what we really needed to do was to get out onto the water ourselves? With this in mind we came up with a plan. By chance Barrie Galpin had been out on a *Rutland Belle* cruise and, while out on the water, he wondered if we should consider taking people out on the large 120-seater boat to try and see fishing Ospreys. John, Tim Appleton and myself agreed that it was a great idea and we approached Trevor Broadhead, the owner of the boat, to see if he would be interested. Trevor agreed to run five trial cruises in 2005.

It was a grey, cold May evening as we left Whitwell Harbour with a group of around 35 passengers on our first ever Osprey cruise. As Trevor took the boat towards the dam we weren't exactly filled with optimism – conditions were hardly tropical. Within a few minutes, though, we picked up our first Osprey. The bird was fishing at the southern end of the dam and, whereas from the shoreline it would have been perhaps half a mile away, with the boat we were able to get much closer. Many fishermen had told us how they'd often seen Ospreys fishing very close to their boats, and now we were experiencing this ourselves. The bird was so intent on fishing that it paid very little attention to us as we gently chugged closer and closer. By the time the bird dived for a fish it was less than 100 metres away. There were gasps of excitement as the bird crashed into the water, then struggled to pull out an enormous trout. With great difficulty it pulled the fish clear of the water and laboured towards the shoreline. A couple of Carrion Crows made life even more difficult and

Introductory talk before an Osprey Cruise.

Passengers on board the Rutland Belle *during an Osprey Cruise. The cruises give visitors the chance of seeing fishing Ospreys at Rutland Water.*

as soon as the bird reached the dam it dropped to the ground and out of sight. The fish was so big there was no chance that it could carry it any further. It would have to be eaten on the ground. We could hardly believe our luck. We hadn't been out on the water for more than half an hour and already we'd enjoyed superb views of a fishing Osprey. There were pats on the back all round, but the fun didn't stop there. We slowly made our way around the eastern end of Rutland Water. Being out on the water gave a sense of scale to the reservoir and views that simply weren't possible from the shoreline. We talked to the excited passengers about the project and the wildlife of the reservoir. It was great fun. After an hour we began to make our way back towards Whitwell Harbour. Another Osprey came into view, this one carrying a fish. It flew almost directly over the boat with its catch, providing incredible views for everyone on board. As the bird flew past us, I noticed Normanton Church in the background. This church was saved when the reservoir was created and it now stands prominently on the southern shoreline. Now we had something to add to that view – an Osprey with a fish. I thought that was a very apt way to end the evening.

As we moored up in the harbour we reflected on what had been a very successful first cruise. The views of the fishing Ospreys had been superb and we knew that this was something we had to continue. Seven summers later, more than 6,000 people have enjoyed Osprey Cruises on the

Rutland Belle. Our evening cruises are now complimented with early morning ones, and people travel from all over the UK to come on them. It's a great way of seeing the reservoir and learning more about these very special birds.

Despite the success of our cruises, we were still hoping for a nest on the reserve. It was great that Site B was proving so successful, but we wanted to share the pleasure of watching an Osprey nest through the breeding season with members of the public. For this reason July 2006 was very significant. 08(97) had spent another lonely summer in Manton Bay but midway through July he was joined by 5N(04). She was the first wild-fledged Rutland female to return but, more significantly from 08(97)'s point of view, she was a female who would not continue north to Scotland the following spring. At last it seemed that he'd found a mate who would stay. 5N(04)'s return next spring – on the day we reopened a refurbished Lyndon Visitor Centre – could hardly have been timed better. The visitor centre at Lyndon was full of people and when Tim Appleton and I went down to Shallow Water Hide to identify 5N(04), the hide was buzzing too. It was a sign of things to come. Over the course of the summer almost 30,000 people visited Lyndon to see the breeding Ospreys. Live images were shown in the visitor centre thanks to a camera installed by our good friend at the Forestry Commission, Jeff Rudd, but it was the views from the hides at Lyndon that were really special.

5R(04) perched close to the Manton Bay nest with the iconic Burley House in the background.

The Manton Bay nest is just a few hundred metres from Waderscrape and Shallow Water Hides, providing some of the best views of breeding Ospreys anywhere in the UK. Each day project volunteers manned high-powered telescopes trained on the nest, and answered questions about the birds. They were able to explain about 08(97)'s repeated attempts to attract a mate and how he'd finally settled down with a 'local bird'. Many visitors remarked that the volunteers greatly enhanced their visit to the reserve. And it worked both ways. Most of the volunteers who helped at Waderscrape Hide that year had previously been involved at Site B, where they had greatly enjoyed the privilege of watching one of only two pairs of breeding Ospreys in England, alone. It's no secret that many were initially reluctant to sign up for shifts at Waderscrape, where volunteering would take on an entirely different focus. Soon though, everyone involved came to really enjoy their shifts at Waderscrape. It is incredibly rewarding to help someone see their first-ever Osprey, whether they are nine years old or 90. In time we found it easier to fill the Waderscrape rota than we did Site B.

Aside from 2009, when 08(97) and 5N(04) moved to Site N, we have had breeding Ospreys on the reserve every year since, and in that time close to 200,000 people have visited specifically to see them. One of the real advances we've made in that period is with the nest camera. In 2010, when 5R(04) took over the nest from his sister, we installed a camera looking directly into the nest for the first time. One of the real highlights of that year was being in the Lyndon Visitor Centre when the first egg hatched and watching the first tender moments as the female offered fish to her newly hatched chick. As on the morning when 5N(04) returned in 2007, the visitor centre was buzzing with excitement, and it didn't stop there. In addition to showing the footage at Lyndon, we also began streaming it onto the project's website. That summer, for the first time, the birds became an international hit. At peak times more than 4,000 people were watching the webcam each day, with individuals logging on from as far afield as North America and Australia. The progress of the Ospreys in Rutland, as well as other places like Cors Dyfi and the Loch of Lowes, was proving compulsive viewing for many. It was great to think

Paul Stammers showing visitors live images from the
Manton Bay nest at the Lyndon Visitor Centre.

Osprey watchers at Waderscrape Hide where visitors are
able to enjoy superb views of the Manton Bay nest.

that people could be doing their ironing while watching
5R(04) delivering a fish to his chicks.

Volunteers have been vital to the running of the project
since day one. In 1996 Helen had a team of just 25 people
to help her, many of whom dedicated huge amounts of time
to monitoring the newly arrived birds. Paul Stammers – who
had just retired – spent in excess of 250 hours huddled in
the tiny monitoring station below the release pens, helping
to record the birds' every move. Since then the number of
volunteers involved in the project has increased year on year.
Now more than 160 people dedicate more than 8,000 hours
to the project every year. Without this kind of dedication it
would simply not be possible to carry out the work we do.

In the early days volunteering very much centred around
the careful monitoring of the translocated birds. As the years
progressed we learnt that recording every single wing-flap
and defecation wasn't essential, but by watching the birds so
intently we grew to know them very well. We quickly picked
up the signs that suggested they were ready for release, we
noted hierarchies that existed within each brood and we got
to know the birds as individuals. If anything was wrong, it

became apparent very quickly. It is probably for this reason
that after the difficulties experienced in 1996, 65 out of 67
birds released in subsequent years set off on migration.

For young people volunteering is a great way of gaining
valuable experience in conservation and for me personally,
it provided the opportunity I needed to make a career out
of my hobby. I still vividly remember my first shift in 'the
outpost', the caravan set at the foot of Lax Hill where we
monitored the translocated birds after release. The sight of
eight newly released Ospreys flying around Lax Hill was
an unforgettable experience. I enjoyed the challenge of
identifying each one by its colour ring and keeping track of
their movements. Little did I know at the time that three
of the birds I was watching that year would have such an
influence on my life in years to come. 03(97) and 08(97)
had just made their first flights and they would later become
two of the most important individuals in the colony. 07(97),
meanwhile, would not return to Rutland after his first
migration, but seven years later I was at his nest site in Mid
Wales and beginning to appreciate what a positive impact the
translocation had had on the distribution of Ospreys in the

An Osprey Family Fun Day at the Lyndon Visitor Centre.

Michelle Househam with a puppet Osprey at a Family Fun Day at Rutland.

UK. I will always be grateful to people like Tim Appleton, Helen McIntyre and Paul Stammers for encouraging me in those early days. I hope that the project is still continuing to give young people the same experiences that I was fortunate enough to enjoy.

Once we had breeding Ospreys in Rutland, volunteering effort switched to monitoring and protecting the breeding birds. From 2002 the focal point of our activities was 03(97)'s nest at Site B. Having positioned a small hide around 250 metres from the nest, volunteers were recruited to guard the nest 24 hours a day. It takes a certain kind of person to forego a night's sleep to protect a pair of breeding Ospreys, but we quickly filled every night shift. Sadly, poor weather resulted in the chick dying soon after hatching, but enthusiasm failed to be dampened by that setback. Next year, when 03(97) attracted a new mate, the volunteers who dedicated time to guarding the nest during incubation were rewarded by the sight of three very healthy chicks. 03(97)

has returned to the nest each spring and over the years we've collected a huge amount of extremely valuable information on Osprey breeding ecology at Site B. Everything from fish deliveries to intruding Ospreys is recorded. Most volunteers are now experts at identifying fish at a distance of more than 250 metres. Site B remains a vitally important nest for the colony and that is why we continue to monitor and protect it.

There's something very satisfying about watching an Osprey nest through the breeding season and I think that's one of the reasons people keep coming back. Where else in today's frantic society do you have the opportunity to sit in one place, with no distractions, for several hours each week? Incubation is not necessarily the most exciting time to be at an Osprey nest, but there is something inherently rewarding about being there – and anyway, all those long hours are rewarded later in the season when things get more interesting. Whether it's watching the female offering fish down into the nest for the first time or watching the juveniles

24th May 09
♀ incubating - site B

making their first flights, there are always memorable moments for volunteers who undertake weekly shifts to enjoy. Their dedication is one of the reasons why the Site B nest has always been so successful.

With the building of a second nest on the nature reserve in 2007 we suddenly had many more shifts to fill. Monitoring two nests 24 hours a day during incubation and then from dawn until dusk later in the season would mean a considerable increase in man-hours. Fortunately, by 2007 our volunteer team had expanded considerably, and everyone rose to the challenge. Many people supplemented their shifts at Site B with one the same day at Manton Bay, and that helped to ensure we had almost constant cover at both nests during the summer. Volunteers also began helping out with Osprey Cruises, guided walks and greeting visitors to the Lyndon Visitor Centre. Each year presented new challenges and new opportunities. There's no doubt that the level of volunteer support we receive helps to make the project the success that it is, but it also greatly enriches the lives of the people involved. Volunteering is a great opportunity to meet like-minded people and to really help make a positive difference. That's exactly what the Rutland Osprey Project volunteers do so superbly well.

Many people have now been involved with the project for a number of years and, having spent so many hours watching breeding Ospreys in Rutland, several volunteers expressed an interest in going to West Africa to see them on their wintering grounds. With that in mind we organised

a trip in January 2011 to some of the key wintering sites in The Gambia and Senegal. The trip was a great success and the two weeks we spent with the volunteers in Africa certainly rank among the most memorable of my time with the project. Our guide Junkung Jadama had only ever had a passing interest in Ospreys before our trip, but by the middle of the second week he too was totally hooked. The trips were such a success that we repeated them in 2012 for another two groups. Apart from providing an opportunity to study Ospreys on their wintering grounds, our time in Africa has given us the chance to develop our education programme and the schools link. This has meant that what was originally planned as a holiday for our volunteers became the inspiration for what we hope will be a long-running and successful education project.

It's not only the general public who have become interested in the project. One of the most rewarding and enjoyable aspects of our work is that it brings us into contact with many of the local landowners, farmers and keepers. As the birds have spread away from Rutland Water we've been fortunate to work with some extremely conscientious and conservation-minded land managers. Many have helped us find sites for new artificial nests, and those who now have breeding Ospreys on their land get just as excited as us when 'their' birds return each spring and then when they come along to ringing later in the season. One local farmer and his wife even joined us on our first trip to West Africa. One of the keys to the long-term success of the project is maintaining these relationships. Our friendships with farmers and keepers have the potential to help a range of other wildlife too. In recent years we've carried out breeding bird surveys and built Barn Owl boxes for a couple of local farmers, and we often advise on how they can incorporate wildlife-friendly practices into their land management. It's only through continuity of staffing and building of relationships that this is possible.

All the evidence points to the fact that flagship species such as Ospreys are vital to conservation. In addition to the interest the Rutland Ospreys have created among members of the public, the local community and landowners, Anglian Water has invested significant funds in the conservation of other, less charismatic species and habitats as a direct result of the success of the Osprey project. Birds like the Osprey can engage with people in a way that few others can. The foresight of a visionary man, George Waterstone, paved the way for the kind of work we're now doing at Rutland Water. The people side of the project has really come to the fore in recent years and with our exciting plans to link communities from Rutland to Africa, we hope our work is having a truly lasting legacy for conservation in the UK and abroad.

THE FUTURE

The success of the Rutland Osprey Project proves the value of proactive conservation. A bird that was once synonymous with remote wild places in northern Scotland is now nesting in the heart of England, within easy reach of millions of people. Our work has completely changed the distribution map of Ospreys in the UK and helped these magnificent birds to return to areas from which they've been absent for centuries. The project also demonstrates the value of conservation and industry working in partnership. The partnership between Anglian Water and the Leicestershire and Rutland Wildlife Trust, which now dates back more than 40 years, is unique and undoubtedly one of the reasons why the project has been such a success.

In years to come we hope that people walking along the banks of the River Thames can look up and see Ospreys close to central London. Whether it's in rural England or fishing villages in The Gambia, the lives of Ospreys are intrinsically linked with our own. They are birds that inspire and enthral and we hope that they're here to stay.

Volunteer Diary, Ken Davies, 2012

A damp, overcast July morning in Rutland County. In villages and towns all around Rutland Water people are up early making preparations for their part in a special series of events – the Olympic torch will be carried through the district today.

Not far from where I am watching the Site B family, villagers go through last-minute routines. Songs, dances and cheers will greet the torch as it's carried through the streets. Crowds will gather, waving flags, blowing trumpets, clapping their hands. This excitement has already lasted more than 40 days and spread the length and breadth of the land, but today it's Rutland's turn. The smallest county in England perhaps, but multum in parvo as the county motto says.

I end my watch at the Site B nest. 'Off to see the torch,' is my final comment in the log. I park outside the village and walk in past people hurrying to find a vantage point for when the torch passes. Here is the school where Osprey Project team members recently took morning assembly and gave the children and teachers a presentation about the Osprey families that live close by. The whole school community will witness the progress of the torch.

Finally we see a white-clad runner bearing the golden torch running towards us, surrounded by guardians and followed by cars and coaches in special Olympic livery. As it passes the flame flickers brightly in the grey sky as the torch-bearer holds it aloft for all to see. In a moment it's gone. The crowds cheer. Some run after it, not wanting to lose the experience so soon. Others start to disperse homewards.

I look up. A distant speck in the sky. An Osprey-watcher is never without a pair of binoculars, but even without them I know which bird it is soaring high over the village as the torch passes through. Broad, strong wings, gleaming white breast and confident circles in the air. A less experienced bird might have mistaken the shining wet road for a winding river or the gilded torch for the glint of a shining fish in the water. But this Osprey, 03(97), is 15 years old, already a nest builder during the 2000 Sydney Olympics, a father of six (including 5R and 5N) by the conclusion of the 2004 Athens Olympics, and of no fewer than 18 by the time the flame was extinguished in Beijing in 2008. That figure will, we hope, have risen to 27 when the London Olympiad reaches its climax in late summer 2012.

Leaning on a wall, I watch him for a long time. My concentrated gaze attracts attention and a small girl, perhaps seven years old and part of a class walking by, asks me what I am looking at. 'It's an Osprey,' I reply. She peers upwards, shielding her eyes. 'Oh yes,' she says 'I see it,' and tells everyone around her. 'You came to our school and told us about the Ospreys,' she adds. She's right, and little does she know how happy and proud she has just made me feel.

Later at Whitwell Creek I see the torch take to the water to Normanton, from where it will resume its land journey out of our county and into Lincolnshire and beyond.

As always I scan the skies. I've already had one Osprey soaring high over the torch procession. Could 5R(04) possibly put in an appearance this afternoon? I fail to spot him but conjure him in my mind, the memory of him stirred by the torch from the year of his birth, 2004, when he and his sister 5N first sailed out from Site B. There is still no sign of him as the flame flickers and falters in the breeze as the boat puts out from the harbour.

How many other Ospreys have been close to the torch as it wends its way through the county today? Perhaps some of our returning band of two-year-olds saw it as they criss-crossed a wide area, revisiting their natal sites or cruising around looking for possible nesting places in years to come? Did 28(10) see it as he revisited his birthplace at Site B? Or 30(10), the young male who first launched from the Manton Bay nest in July 2010? And then there's that young female 25(10), daughter of AW(06) and hatched at Site O – did the torch catch her attention as she moved through her old haunts? I like to think so.

The last time we had an Olympiad in the UK was in 1948, when there had been no breeding Ospreys in England for nearly a hundred years, and there were none in Scotland apart from the occasional vagrant. Rutland Water didn't exist. Sixty-four years later we have a developing colony in central England, over 220 pairs in Scotland, and small numbers becoming established in Wales and northern England.

If we have to wait six or seven decades for another UK Olympics, how many pairs of Ospreys will we have by then? It will be up to that little girl who witnessed the torch passing and saw an Osprey soaring over her village, and thousands of children like her, to grow up and continue to value and protect their environment and everything living in it. If they do, then Ospreys, like the Olympics, could go on forever.

Where to Watch Ospreys at Rutland Water

The best place to see Ospreys at Rutland Water is the Lyndon Visitor Centre, situated off the minor road on the south shore of the reservoir, midway between the villages of Manton and Edith Weston. The centre is open daily from 9am to 5pm from March to September. Live images from the Manton Bay nest are shown on a big screen in the centre, and staff and volunteers from the project are on hand to answer your questions. Waderscrape Hide, a 15-minute walk from the visitor centre, offers excellent views of the Osprey nest and is also manned by Rutland Osprey Project volunteers with telescopes to help you get the best possible view of the birds.

The reserve's other visitor centre at Egleton offers the chance of Osprey sightings as well as excellent birding throughout the year.

ON THE WEB

Keep up to date with all the latest news from the project at www.ospreys.org.uk.

Each summer more than 30,000 people visit the Lyndon Visitor Centre to see the live images relayed there from the Manton Bay Osprey nest. The hides that overlook this nest are only a 15-minute walk from the centre, through the nature reserve's traditionally managed hay meadows.

References

Dennis, R. H. 2008 *A Life of Ospreys*. Whittles Publishing, Dunbeath.
Fray, R., Davies, R., Gamble, D., Harrop A. & Lister, S. 2009. *The Birds of Leicestershire and Rutland*. Christopher Helm, London.
Haines, C. R. 1907 *Notes on the Birds of Rutland*. R. H. Porter, London.
Mitcham, T. 1984 *The Birds of Rutland and its Reservoirs*. Sycamore Press Ltd, Wymondham.
Zwarts, L., Bijlsma, R., van der Kamp, J. & Wymenga, E. 2009 *Living on the Edge: Wetlands and Birds in a Changing Sahel*. KNNV Publishing, the Netherlands.

Acknowledgements

The success of the Rutland Osprey project is down to the input of so many people, not least the hundreds of volunteers who have dedicated over 100,000 hours to monitoring the birds and helping visitors to enjoy seeing them since the first birds were translocated in 1996. The project would simply not be possible without their enthusiasm, dedication and enduring commitment.

We are indebted, too, to the landowners who have allowed us access to their land to monitor breeding Ospreys and to erect artificial nests. Sadly, and for obvious reasons, we cannot mention them individually here, but their support has been vital to the success of the project.

The 40-year partnership between Anglian Water and the Leicestershire and Rutland Wildlife Trust at Rutland Water is an outstanding example of conservation and industry working together. Anglian Water's funding and continued support of the project is vital and we are extremely grateful to them for that. Particular thanks are due to Stephen Bolt for helping to get the project off the ground in the mid-90s and to Andy Brown for his ongoing support.

We had been talking for some time about writing a book on the project, but we are extremely grateful to Kay Coleman-Rooney, formerly of Anglian Water, who gave the idea new impetus.

Roy Dennis has been an inspirational figure in UK conservation for the last 50 years and the project would not have been possible without his involvement and unwavering support.

Finally thanks to everyone at Bloomsbury, particularly Julie Bailey, for helping us to produce what we think is a fine representation of almost 20 years of hard work, and to Sara Hulse and Julie Dando for their editing and design expertise respectively.

Image Credits

Index

Pagination in *italic* refers to illustration captions

Leicestershire
& Rutland
Wildlife Trust

The Leicestershire and Rutland Wildlife Trust is justifiably proud of the successes and achievements of the Rutland Osprey project and the key role it has played in the Trust's work to protect and enhance the wildlife and wild places of Leicestershire and Rutland and to engage people with their local environment.

Far more than just a conservation success story, the Rutland Osprey Project has also enabled many thousands of people of all ages to see these magnificent birds close up, whether in the wonderful environs of Rutland Water or logging on to the project website and watching stunning webcam images of one of the nests.

Leicestershire and Rutland Wildlife Trust has managed Rutland Water Nature Reserve since its creation in the mid-1970s working in partnership with Anglian Water. The Rutland Osprey Project further underlines the strength and importance of this remarkable and longstanding collaboration between conservation and industry. Long may it continue!

Simon Bentley

Director, Leicestershire and Rutland Wildlife Trust

Anglian Water's region has fantastic wildlife, with a wealth of habitats that are home to a host of rare plants and animals. Many of our own sites, just like Rutland Water, are nationally and internationally important for the wildlife that they sustain.

Our belief has always been that we should do more that just conserve the wildlife at these sites; we should work with others to enhance it. Our partnership with the Leicestershire and Rutland Wildlife Trust, the reserve staff and all the volunteers at Rutland Water has been a shining example of this over the last 40 years.

I am immensely proud of what we have all achieved at Rutland Water, the pinnacle of which is restoring a strong breeding population of ospreys to the heart of England after an absence of 150 years. I hope that everyone who visits the reservoir and enjoys seeing these glorious birds above the water, or who reads this account of their return, is left with a feeling that, when we work together, we can make a positive impact on our environment. My thanks go out to all of those who gave, and still give, their time to help us make this happen.

Andy Brown

Head of Sustainability, Anglian Water

Rutland Water Nature Reserve

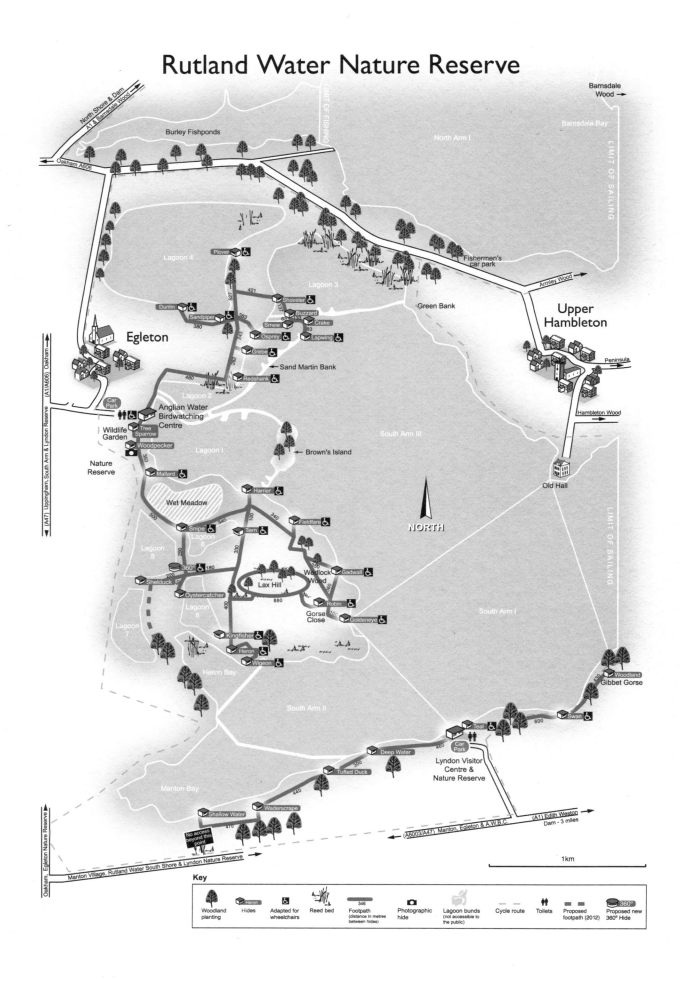

North Shore & Dam
A1 & Barnsdale Wood

Barnsdale Wood →

Barnsdale Bay

← Oakham A606

Burley Fishponds

North Arm I

LIMIT OF SAILING

LIMIT OF FISHING

Lagoon 4

Plover

Lagoon 3

Fishermen's car park

Armley Wood →

Egleton

421

Dunlin

587

Shoveler

Green Bank

Upper Hambleton

Sandpiper

363

380

243

Smew

Buzzard

65

137

Crake

83

Peninsula →

Osprey

Lapwing

Grebe

282

Sand Martin Bank

(A1/A606) Oakham

Car Park

480

Redshank

Lagoon 2

Hambleton Wood →

Anglian Water Birdwatching Centre

South Arm III

Wildlife Garden

Tree Sparrow

Woodpecker

363

Lagoon 1

Brown's Island

(A47) Uppingham, South Arm & Lyndon Reserve

Mallard

Old Hall

Nature Reserve

Wet Meadow

Harrier

550

100

340

Fieldfare

NORTH

Snipe

340

Tern

LIMIT OF SAILING

Lagoon 6

290

330

Lagoon 5

360°

180

Wedlock Wood

Gadwall

390

360

Shelduck

220

Lax Hill

Robin

South Arm I

Oystercatcher

400

880

Gorse Close

100

Lagoon 8

Goldeneye

Lagoon 7

Kingfisher

Heron

Wigeon

Woodland

Gibbet Gorse

480

Heron Bay

South Arm II

600

Swan

Teal

Car Park

Deep Water

Lyndon Visitor Centre & Nature Reserve

440

300

Tufted Duck

(A1) Edith Weston
Dam - 3 miles

Manton Bay

Shallow Water

470

Waderscrape

(A6003/A47) Manton, Egleton & A.W.B.C.

No access beyond this point

Egleton Nature Reserve

Manton Village, Rutland Water South Shore & Lyndon Nature Reserve →

Oakham,

1km

Key

| Woodland planting | Hides (Heron) | Adapted for wheelchairs | Reed bed | Footpath (distance in metres between hides) 346 | Photographic hide | Lagoon bunds (not accessible to the public) | Cycle route | Toilets | Proposed footpath (2012) | Proposed new 360° Hide |